Charlottenburg Palace

P9-DEN-000

MUSEEN
SCHLÖSSER
und DENKMÄLER
in DEUTSCHLAND

directed by Thomas W. Gaehtgens

CHARLOTTENBURG PALACE, BERLIN

edited by Winfried and Ilse Baer

with contributions by Winfried Baer
Renate L. Colella
Tilo Eggeling
Thomas Kemper

FONDATION PARIBAS

Contents

Andreas Schlüter (1659–1714)
Equestrian statue of Friedrich Wilhelm, the Great
Elector (1640–88)
Bronze, 1699–1708
The statue was commissioned by Friedrich I and
installed on the Lange Brücke near the Royal Palace in
1703. Having been removed for safety during the
Second World War, it was discovered submerged in
the Tegeler See in 1949, and in 1952 it was installed
in the main courtyard at Charlottenburg.

(Cover)
Charlottenburg Palace, garden façade

(Frontispiece)
Charlottenburg Palace (1695–1713), front view (south
side), showing the main building by Johann Arnold
Nering (1659–95) and the cupola added by Johann
Friedrich Eosander (known as Göthe; 1669–1728).
In the middle of the main courtyard is the equestrian
statue of Friedrich Wilhelm the Great Elector.

Introduction

 efore the last war, Berlin still boasted a whole collection of palaces. However, only five of these had the kind of historical importance, architectural quality, and outstanding decoration to merit supervision by the Administration of State Palaces and Gardens.

Heading the list was the Royal Palace, located in the heart of the city. It was the oldest of the Hohenzollerns' royal residences, and the richest in tradition, dating back to the fifteenth century. With its 1,200 rooms it was also the largest and most imposing of the palaces, and from 1927, it was the headquarters of the Administration of State Palaces and Gardens. Next on the list was Charlottenburg Palace (Lietzenburg), especially renowned for its huge grounds. Then came Monbijou Palace, for many years the home of Queen Sophie Dorothea, wife of the 'Soldier King', Friedrich Wilhelm I. All three palaces were badly damaged during the war, but there was scope for reconstruction. However, for purely ideological reasons, what was left of the two buildings that lay in East Berlin – that is to say, the Royal Palace and Monbijou – were blown up on the orders of the GDR leadership: all memory of the Hohenzollern dynasty had to be erased, here in the heart of the city. Charlottenburg Palace, located in West Berlin, escaped this fate and was rebuilt over a period of many years.

Because of the destruction of the other buildings, notably the Royal Palace, Charlottenburg acquired a special status amongst the surviving Hohenzollern residences in Berlin and Brandenburg. It is now the only royal palace in which all the kings of Prussia lived or resided at one time or another. In most cases, this also means that buildings were added or alterations made by the monarchs, so that what we have is a record of court life covering the period from 1695, when Electress Sophie Charlotte laid the foundation stone, until the late nineteenth-century imperial age.

Once the Royal Palace had been destroyed, Charlottenburg took its place, and had to accommodate important

items from its stock of furnishings. The peregrination of movables from one Hohenzollern palace to another was thoroughly in keeping with tradition: if the king moved his court from one place to another, or if crowned heads were accommodated in a particular palace during a visit to Berlin, the furnishings were often supplemented by stocks from other palaces. Many paintings and items of furniture still bear the inventory marks of several palaces.

The focal point of the Charlottenburg interior will always be the age of Sophie Charlotte and her consort, Friedrich I. It was they who contributed most to the emergence of this imposing royal site.

Winfried Baer

Earliest view of Schloß Lietzenburg (main front) after a plan by Johann Arnold Nering (1659–95). The building was formally opened on 1 July 1699 Engraving from: Lorenz Beger, *Thesaurus Brandenburgicus*, III, c. 1696

Eastern wall of the Porcelain Chamber

7

The Electress Sophie Charlotte

ophie Charlotte was the second wife of the electoral heir Friedrich of Brandenburg. They were married in 1684, after the death of Friedrich's first wife, Elisabeth Henriette. Sophie Charlotte was the daughter of Duke Ernst August of Braunschweig-Lüneburg (1629–1698; first elector of Hanover from 1692) and his wife, Sophie (1630–1714). As the daughter of Friedrich V of the Palatinate (1596–1632) – the 'Winter King' – and of Elizabeth Stuart (1596–1662), who herself was daughter of James I of England, Sophie was keen to achieve dynastic advancement. The period of brilliance to which she owes her name in European history began when she was electress of Hanover. In 1701, the British Parliament's Act of Settlement had declared the electress-widow of Hanover and granddaughter of the Stuart king heir to the English throne. In 1714, her son – Sophie Charlotte's brother – assumed the British throne as George I.

Many of Sophie's qualities – dignity, intelligence, virtue – were also to be found in her daughter. As the wife of Friedrich III, Sophie Charlotte spent a considerable part of the year in Hanover and Herrenhausen, where she occupied the 'Prussian rooms' which her mother kept ready for her. It was between these two poles of attraction – Lietzenburg and Hanover – that most of Sophie Charlotte's life was spent.

The cultivation of music at the parental court in Braunschweig later proved of great value to Sophie Charlotte. Her brilliant technique on the cembalo, acquired under the tutorship of Anton Coberg, earned her much admiration at Versailles. Later, in Lietzenburg – what is today Charlottenburg – she occasionally also directed performances of opera from the cembalo. She had the same detestation as her mother for the loud playing of the royal trumpets and kettle-drums which were part of the daily ceremonial at her husband's Berlin court. Like her brother Georg Ludwig (later George I of Britain), she was a passionate admirer of chamber music; however, since her means were insufficient to allow her her own orchestra, she depended mostly on 'borrowed musicians'. Music at Lietzenburg flourished 'on quality and the intimate charm of solo performers or small ensembles'.

Italian musicians played an outstanding role at the young electress's court. In 1696 these included the singer and opera-composer Francesco Antonio Pistocchi and the highly regarded violinist, composer for violin, and concertmaster Giuseppe Torelli, both on loan from Margrave Georg Friedrich of Ansbach, a friend of Sophie Charlotte's. The renowned musician Agostino Steffani, who was at one time director of the new opera-house in Hanover, proved a true friend to Sophie Charlotte in a number of ways.

In a letter to him on 21 November 1702, she says of music that 'It is a loyal friend;

Commemorative medal with bust of the Electress Sophie Charlotte by Johann Bernhard Schulz (d. 1695, employed at the Berlin mint from 1685)
Silver, diam. 47 mm
Berlin, c. 1690

Friedrich Wilhelm Weidemann (1668–1750)
Sophie Charlotte (1668–1705), Queen in Prussia
Oil on canvas, 1702–5

Anton Schoonjans (c. 1655–1726)
Attilio Ariosti
The Italian musician and composer Attilio Ariosti,
a monk of the Servite Order, was employed, with the
special dispensation of his Order, at Sophie
Charlotte's court from 1697 to 1703.
Oil on canvas, 1702

Anton Schoonjans (c. 1655–1726)
Battista Buononcini
Musical life at Sophie Charlotte's court came into full
flower under Battista Buononcini, though he was
resident for only one year (1702–3) at Charlottenburg.
Oil on canvas, 1702

it does not let you down or deceive you; it is not a traitor and is never cruel. No: it gives you all the charms and delights of heaven, whereas friends are indifferent or deceitful, and loved ones ungrateful.' Steffani was particularly supportive to her when she set up the small opera-house in Lietzenburg. It was inaugurated, with a performance of a comedy and an opera, on 5 August 1699, on the occasion of the marriage of the electoral heir, Friedrich Wilhelm (I), to Sophie Dorothea of Braunschweig-Lüneburg. The libretto was by the Hanover-based librettist Abbate Ortensio Mauro. The programme came under the overall direction of Attilio Ariosti, a viola-d'amore player and singer who was employed as an opera-composer at Lietzenburg between 1697 and 1703. The queen owned a portrait of this renowned musician, a monk of the Servite Order, whose services she had requested from the Duke of Mantua. Another portrait in the Charlottenburg Palace shows the Modena-born Giovanni Battista Buononcini, composer at the Viennese court, who worked at Lietzenburg between 1702 and 1703 and evidently brought along a choir. It was at Lietzenburg that he wrote the famous opera *Polifemo*. With Ariosti, he was later to become a fierce rival of Handel's in London.

The ten-year predominance of Italian music at Lietzenburg ended with the period of service of the composer Ruggiero Fedeli, released a second time from his duties by the Landgrave of Hessen-Kassel and sent to Lietzenburg. It was he who eventually wrote the music for Sophie Charlotte's funeral on 28 June 1705.

As a particularly precious reminder of the queen's musical passion, two Chinese lacquered cembali have been placed on display in Charlottenburg Palace. They are attributed to the Berlin court instrument-maker Michael Mietke.

Given Sophie Charlotte's untimely death, the huge construction that makes up baroque Charlottenburg is not all her own work; much of it is due to Friedrich I. But the intellectual charisma she radiated was hers alone. It was thanks to her good offices that the polymath and greatest German scholar of the time, Gottfried Wilhelm Leibniz (1646–1716), came to Berlin. With her help, he was able to realize his dream of an Academy of Sciences in Berlin, which was duly founded in 1700 by Elector Friedrich III. Sophie Charlotte, who arranged a room for Leibniz at Lietzenburg in that year, became his chief intellectual companion.

Between 1698 and 1711, Berlin became Leibniz's major place of work, alongside Hanover. This outstanding scholar – with whom Sophie Charlotte formed deep ties of friendship – thus also acted as Hanover's political representative in Berlin. During these few years, the electress and the philosopher together made scientific history.

The historian Leopold von Ranke (1795–1886) describes Sophie Charlotte as follows: 'Her peculiar talent – perhaps the one most suited to the mature female intellect – was conversation. In complete contrast to her husband, who rose extremely early and liked to punctuate his daily labours with ceremonial splendour, she liked long evenings, informality, unconstrained conversation. No kind of flattery, still less any kind of ugliness, would have been allowed anywhere near her; she could tell the true from the false. The scholars whom she drew to her never forgot that combination of beauty and intellect, nobility and civility, which she embodied. She seems to have been the same with those who made up the court. She knew her people through and through, and spared none of their traits in private conversation; arrogance, particularly of a maladroit kind, she would dismiss icily; what she encouraged instead was bashful modesty. She was proud and full of grace.'

WB

Second Haute-Lisse Room, Sophie Charlotte's audience chamber at the time of the original construction of the palace (1695–9). The walls are decorated with three tapestries from a series of 'Watteau scenes' by the Berlin workshop of Charles Vigne, *c.* 1740. The cembalo, belonging to Sophie Charlotte, was made by the Berlin court instrument-maker Michael Mietke (*c.* 1665–before 1729). The colourful painting in Chinese style on a white-lacquer ground is attributed to Gerard Dagly (1657–1726), *c.* 1700.

Elector Friedrich III

lector Friedrich III (1657–1713) – first 'king in Prussia' (Friedrich I) from 1701 – was the son of Friedrich Wilhelm the Great Elector (1620–1688) and his consort Louisa Henrietta of Orange (1627–1667). Being frail by nature, and deformed as a result of a fracture of the spine, Friedrich remained very much in the shadow of his elder brother, Karl Emil, who died in 1673. His father paid him little regard, and Friedrich's youth was marked by distrust of his father and of his stepmother, Dorothea. His tutor and long-time confidant, Eberhard Danckelmann, obtained high office once Friedrich succeeded to the electorate in 1688.

Friedrich's second marriage, to Sophie Charlotte of Braunschweig-Lüneburg (1668–1705), was a dynastically motivated union. Sophie Charlotte's ties with Hanover resulted in a tense relationship with Danckelmann, whose fall she was instrumental in procuring in 1697.

Despite unfavourable preconditions, Friedrich III developed into an important actor on the political stage, and managed, for all his military commitments abroad, to preserve peace in his own country. Opposing the stipulations of his father's will, which provided for a share of the inheritance to go to Friedrich's half-brother, Friedrich managed to enforce the right of primogeniture, thus preserving territorial and administrative unity in Brandenburg. He also succeeded in checking Louis XIV's primacy in Europe by pursuing a policy of unity between Protestants and Catholics in his realm. The same objective lay behind his powerful support for William III of Orange in the struggle against the combined might of James II and Louis XIV for the English crown (the 'Glorious Revolution').

Despite the successful role thus played by Brandenburg as an auxiliary European power in the Netherlands, and along the Rhine, Po, and Danube, Friedrich III was obliged, in the Peace of Ryswick of 1697, to acknowledge Brandenburg's lack of an autonomous status amongst the European princedoms. This bitter experience strengthened him in his resolve to secure a crown – all the more so since the elector of Saxony had obtained the Polish crown, the Guelphs had their eye on the English throne, and the Wittelsbachs harboured intermittent ambitions in regard to the Spanish crown.

As a representative of the Baroque, Friedrich equipped the office of king with all the trappings of magnificence then available: more than twenty summer residences sprang up around Berlin; and in the city itself, the Hohenzollern castle, which had grown up over centuries, was transformed by Andreas Schlüter (1644–1714) into the most imposing and remarkable baroque palace in northern Europe. Jean-Baptiste Colbert's notion that monarchs must demonstrate their greatness and importance by what they build, is particularly apposite to Friedrich. He used his palace construction as continual visible proof of his kingship.

Leibniz, whose move to Berlin had been mediated by Sophie Charlotte, had long cherished the dream of a 'Germanic Societie of Sciences'. On 11 June 1770, the elector granted him his wish (the society subsequently became the Prussian Academy of Sciences). Leibniz was later to assure Friedrich that, as elector of Brandenburg, he had had all the qualities of a king.

Although Sophie Charlotte's relations with her husband were circumspect and distant, and although her heart always lay more with Hanover than with Brandenburg, Friedrich none the less had a genuine affection for her, despite their very different characters. Lietzenburg – later Charlottenburg – is, as we shall see, particularly eloquent testimony to that.

WB

Antoine Pesne (1683–1757)
Friedrich I in Coronation Robes
Oil on canvas, *c.* 1710

The Beginnings of Electress Sophie Charlotte's Summer Residence

he first palace which Elector Friedrich III made over to his wife Sophie Charlotte, on 24 August 1690, was Haus Caputh, on the shores of the Schielow lake (near Potsdam). He had bought the house from the heirs of his stepmother, the widowed Electress Dorothea, who had died in 1689. The palace which the young electress received had been built by Philippe de Chièze in 1662 and extended in 1673, and it had a small garden on the side overlooking the lake. On 5 June 1694, however, she gave the property back, because of its 'considerable distance from the electoral residence' in Berlin. Her choice fell instead on the large, undeveloped area west of the Tiergarten, along the River Spree and close to the village of Lütze – also known as 'Lützow' or 'Lietze' – which was easy to reach both by water and by road.

The history of the first palace of Lietzenburg which is mentioned for the first time by this name in 1695, has never been properly recorded.

The much-sought-after Dutch architect Arnold Nering was appointed 'Superintendent of All Our Buildings' by Elector Friedrich III on 9 April 1691. On 21 October 1695, however, shortly before construction started at Lietzenburg, Nering died. The task was immediately passed to the structural engineer Martin Grünberg, who also took over responsibility for the continuation of Nering's work on the other electoral building-projects. In 1698 the elector transferred Grünberg's supervisory responsibilities for the building of the Berlin Zeughaus (arsenal), also begun by Nering, to his court sculptor, Andreas Schlüter, and in that same year he charged Schlüter with the preparatory work for the alterations to the Royal Palace. It is therefore likely that this renowned baroque artist was also involved in the creation of Lietzenburg. The literature of the eighteenth century always attributed the early design of the palace to Schlüter, but more recent art-history is divided on this. In his latest investigations, Goerd Peschken advances the thesis – in many respects well founded – that Schlüter was in charge of the building-work between 1698 and 1701, in the footsteps of Grünberg. Peschken rightly classifies Grünberg as being predominantly an engineer, not qualified to assume the responsibilities of a royal architect.

What Sophie Charlotte had initially commissioned was a *maison de plaisance*, a small summer-palace to which one could escape from the constraints of official etiquette for a few hours during the warm months of the year.

The core of this first palace still nestles inside the jutting central portion of the extended baroque construction. A series of plans and views from the early days give us a vivid picture of Nering's building, and of the later architectural additions and extensions.

Ceiling of a room in the Mecklenburg Apartment
In the centre is a painting on canvas depicting *Venus in Triumphal Chariot being Crowned by Graces*. During the 19th century, the small rooms east of the cupola and overlooking the main courtyard became known as the Mecklenburg Rooms because the royal relations from Mecklenburg used to lodge here.

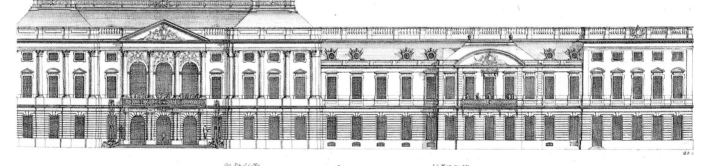

Façade du Palais Royal de Charlottebourg.

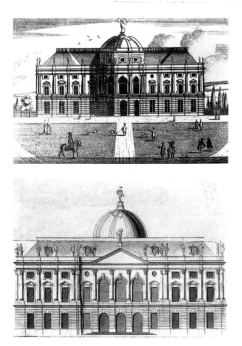

View based on an elevation of the garden front drawn as part of the plans for reconstruction of the pavilion
Engraving from: John Tolland, *Relation des cours de Prusse et de Hanovre*, before 1702

View of main façade
Anonymous wash drawing, before 1702
Former State Archive, Dresden, destroyed by fire 1944

This first version of Lietzenburg was fully in keeping with the fashion of the day for having small-scale palaces set out on their own in the countryside, a favoured site being on the periphery of royal capitals. The palace has come down to us as a compact, rigorous, self-contained structure with two storeys and a mezzanine. The long side was divided into eleven bays, and the short side into four. The ground-floor façade, decorated with banded rustication, was sectioned by pilasters that continued into the two upper floors as Corinthian half-columns. The courtyard façade, which faced south, comprised three compartments, the five-bayed centre of which was set back by one bay. The outer bays of these portions of the façade served as optical 'hinges' between the side-projections and the projecting porchway, with its accentuating frontispiece and triple arcade. Echoing these portals on the upper storey were large, round-arched windows that took in the mezzanine. The middle-storey windows on the side of the building were picked out with 'eared' frames and alternating pointed and segmental gables, in the manner of a *bel étage*. The projections were terminated at the side with cross-corner half-columns. On some of the views of the palace, the middle segmental gables on the side projections are further enhanced by matching pairs of reclining figures with additional side-decoration. The ledge (attic) above it was topped with figures. The steep hipped roof ended at the top in a flat roof-terrace surrounded by railings.

The garden side repeats this division into three, but the middle projection is replaced by a three-storey, elliptical projecting pavilion, only three of whose five windows are visible from the front. The cupola, which would have continued the mural divisions in the form of relief ribbing, was to have been topped by a tall statue of Fortuna, which would have served as a weathervane. This cupola, set on a low, mezzanine-style tambour and appearing at varyingly sharp angles on a number of different illustrations, was probably never built, because it does not figure in the 1701 view in Pitzler's sketchbook.

The ultimate inspiration for these 'pavilion' designs was Gianlorenzo Bernini's original plan for the eastern façade of the Louvre in Paris, which provided for the first time for a projecting central pavilion. Considerably better known at that time, however, were the central pavilions of the *maisons de plaisance* at Vaux-le-Vicomte and Raincy, designed by Louis Levau. At about the same time as Charlottenburg was being built, Fischer von Erlach in Vienna was also trying out variations on this theme. On the ground floor, the projecting façade at Lietzenburg enclosed a *salle à l'italienne*, through the glass doors of which the visitor could glimpse the garden from the courtyard side. Despite the various architectural changes, this is still possible today. Over the top of this was the palace's main banqueting-hall.

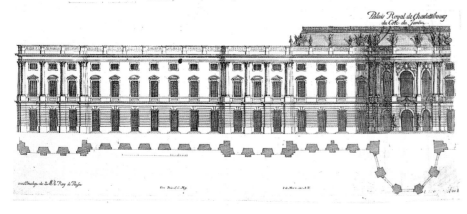

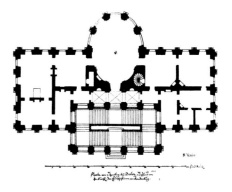

Jean-Baptiste Broebes (c. 1660–1720)
Plans for an extension of the Nering building,
c. 1698–9
Engravings from *Vues des Palais et Maisons de
Plaisance de S. M. le Roy de Prusse*, Augsburg, 1733

Nicodemus Tessin the Younger (1654–1728)
Plan of ground floor of the main building, with design
for central stairway, c. 1698
Stockholm, Nationalmuseum

The first incentive for an extension of the palace came when Nicodemus Tessin the Younger (1654–1728) – architect to Charles XI of Sweden and pupil of Gianlorenzo Bernini and Carlo Fontana – who was then beginning the construction of the northern wing of the palace in Stockholm, had the idea of building a central stairway. His plans for Lietzenburg envisaged a grandiose two-way angled staircase inside the *grande corniche* or entrance recess. The French architect Jean-Baptiste Broebes (c. 1660–1720), a pupil of Daniel Marot, whilst serving as military engineer in Berlin, had produced plans and views of royal palaces many of which were ingenious amalgamations of his own and other architects' ideas. He incorporated a modified version of the Tessin stairway into a fascinating view of the palace which also included a large railed courtyard, side arcades with balustraded terraces, and two separate one-storey transverse buildings. An extension of this kind was thus evidently under consideration at that time. The changes indicated in these plans show Lietzenburg's gradual evolution from a *maison de plaisance* to a royal residence with its own household.

For the mistress of the works, the proximity of her own rooms to the garden had absolute priority. These were therefore located, not on the *piano nobile* or upper storey, as might have been supposed from outside, but on the ground floor. In 1701 Pitzler reported that the windows on the garden side reached down to the ground, so that each room had direct access to the garden. As in the case of many such *maisons de plaisance*, the accommodation was limited: two largish square apartments on either side of the very homely *salla terrena*, with its many pictures, both began with an antechamber. On the eastern side this then connected to a Bedroom, and on the west side to the Audience Chamber. On the courtyard side, with no intervening corridor, only concealed doors leading straight into the garden suite, there was a series of smaller rooms. One of these was the Porcelain Chamber, which probably also served as a dressing-room. The queen's Study was located on the west side.

The walls of the Oval Hall on the upper floor were sectioned off by Corinthian pilasters, as shown today; and the five window-arches in the front half of the oval were echoed by five mirrored recesses in the back half. Much effort was expended in re-creating this arrangement after the last war. Connecting to the Hall were the apartments of Margrave Albrecht Friedrich of Brandenburg-Schwedt (1672–1731) – an admirer of Sophie Charlotte's, who in 1703 celebrated his marriage to the princess of Kurland in Charlottenburg – and the rooms of Princess Ludovica Dorothea of Kassel, the queen's stepdaughter. The new rooms adjoining on the courtyard side included the apartments of Crown Prince Friedrich Wilhelm (I).

17

'Glass Bedchamber' looking south-east
The name of this room, which was in use in Sophie
Charlotte's time, derives from the slender strips of
mirror that alternate with green damask on the walls.
Beaded chandelier: France, c. 1700

'Glass Bedchamber' looking south-west
Photo: Meßbildanstalt, c. 1915

Antoine Pesne (1683–1757)
Margrave Albrecht Friedrich von Brandenburg-
Schwedt (1672–1731), Stepbrother to Friedrich I,
Oil on canvas, c. 1720

Antechamber to the 'Glass Bedchamber'
The ceiling painting by Augustin Terwesten (1649–
1711) was lost during the war; the richly gilded stucco
decoration on the ceiling was restored in 1973.

On the mezzanine there were rooms for the ladies-in-waiting and also two furniture rooms.

These rooms suffered a lot of damage in 1943. The plaster on the already flat ceilings had been decorated with, again, a flattish relief of acanthus and palm motifs. In line with long-established tradition, the ceiling coffers were themselves divided into a large number of smaller sections. In 1698, the court painter and academy director Augustin Terwesten the Elder (1649–1711), working with his brother Matthias, covered the greater part of the ceiling surface with canvases; and in the side panels, *grisaille* paintings were executed straight onto the plaster. The pictures in the electress's ground-floor rooms were devoted to the themes of 'Venus' and 'Cupid and Psyche', the two surviving ones in the two upper rooms at the western end of the Hall to 'Apollo' and 'Jupiter'.

A special feature of Lietzenburg was its 'mirror chambers', probably created under Dutch influence. Such chambers were intended to open up the walls optically and draw nature – the garden – into the room. Both the Porcelain Chamber, with its red panelling and three sets of cross-corner mirrored shelving, on which stood about 430 items of East Asian porcelain and Delft faïence, and the Glass Bedchamber were corner rooms and therefore had two external walls, which meant that more light and more greenery entered the room. Until 1943, the Bedchamber, which has now been restored, was regarded as one of the best-preserved rooms of the early palace-building. It was decorated with lengths of grass-green floral damask alternating with strips of mirror. It is one of the earliest examples of a type of room later to be found in a large number of palaces. The chimney wall is based on a design by Daniel Marot.

An inspection of the oldest inventory of Charlottenburg – dating from 1705 and one of the most important sources of information on the early palace – shows that the furniture comprised a large number of writing-desks, tables, *guéridons*, and various boxes that were lacquered and are described as 'Indian' because of their East Asian style. The name 'Dagly' crops up in this connection. Gérard Dagly, a native of the famous health-resort of Spa, near Aachen, had come to Berlin in the Great Elector's day, and since 1696 had held the post of Intendant des Ornaments. In the same year, he obtained a patent on the production of 'Japanese' lacquer. Although he worked only with varnish, Dagly must have been an outstanding master of his craft, because the Duchesse d'Orléans actually assumed there was an 'Indian' – in other words a Chinese or Japanese craftsman – working in Berlin. The hallmark of Dagly's work, as one can still see today, was his brilliant imitation – particularly from the point of view of style – of Japanese lacquerwork, for which there were plenty of models available in the various palaces. The famous white cembalo belonging to Sophie Charlotte was probably produced in the Dagly workshop.

A distinguishing feature of the many furnishings that have survived from the early days of Charlottenburg is, as in other domains, their international character: in addition to items produced in Berlin, and to Chinese and Japanese lacquered furniture, there are also Dutch, English, and French furnishings, as well as a secretary desk from Antwerp.

The collection of paintings that had been assembled by the time of Sophie Charlotte's death in 1705 comprised mainly portraits, many of them contemporary. These portraits of visitors to Charlottenburg, or of people with whom the queen was in contact, hung in serried ranks in the various rooms. The ground-floor hall, accommodating as it did eighty pictures, must have looked as if it had

Large octagonal red-lacquered drum-table with gold decoration, Audience Chamber
Java, c. 1680
Base: Berlin, c. 1680

Carved and gilded showpiece-table with *pietra dura*-style painting of Friedrich I's monogram and the black Prussian eagle, 'Glass Bedchamber'
Berlin, 1705–13

Black-lacquered cupboard with gold painting (on the outside) and Chinese motifs against a white ground (on the inside), Audience Chamber
Berlin, Gerard Dagly workshop, *c.* 1700

Black-lacquered cupboard with gold painting and mother-of-pearl inlay, Audience Chamber
Japan, during transition from Momoyama to Edo Period, *c.* 1630
Base: Berlin, end 17th century
From the Kunstkammer in the Royal Palace

Black-lacquer cabinet with gold painting and elaborately carved and gilded base
England, *c.* 1690

'Indian Writing-Desk', lacquered white and painted. From Queen Sophie Charlotte's Study
Antwerp, end 17th century

Dressing Room in Sophie Charlotte's Second Apartment, *c.* 1702, looking in a south-westerly direction
The red and green brocade wall-covering is new.

been 'paved' with them, given that there were not only five large window-arches but also three double folding doors.

The queen's Bedchamber in her 'Second Apartment' contained a collection of fifty-five Dutch landscapes, floral paintings, genre scenes, and mythological and religious paintings. The decorative effect of these clustered collections of pictures was further enhanced by the sumptuous 'carved and gilded' frames.

The most radical developments in construction work at Lietzenburg began after Friedrich's coronation at Königsberg (18 January 1701). At the beginning of 1701, supervision of the building-works was taken over by the Swedish architect Johan Friedrich d'Eosander, known as Göthe (1669–1729), who had been appointed Court Architect in Berlin in 1699, having first been sent on study tours to Italy and France. He proved to be a skilful decorator for the theatre and for state events, and this may have been what aroused Sophie Charlotte's interest. There are also records of his supervising construction work at the palaces of Schönhausen, Oranienburg, and Monbijou. After Schlüter's disaster with the Münzturm, Eosander succeeded him as supervisor of works at the Royal Palace.

In December 1701, Göthe presented some new plans and 'un grand et beau modèle' at Lietzenburg, news of which was sent to Hanover by Leibniz on 3 January. As far as Sophie Charlotte was concerned, Göthe would be 'the oracle as regards all her building affairs'. This was how she described him to her mother in a letter of 18 May 1702. That spring saw the start of the large-scale extension works. Eosander's design, preserved in a large-scale bird's-eye view of the palace site, presented the plans for a continuous, three-winged building (with a main courtyard closed off by railings) in systematic form. The transverse wings, punctuated by projections, were given added emphasis in the shape of terminal buildings at the ends facing the road. Eosander extended the garden front of the old *corps de logis* by adding seven new sections at the same height in both directions, such that the building spanned the whole width of the formal garden. This façade, rhythmically sectioned by its four flat projections, bears an unmistakable resemblance to the garden façade at Versailles, which Eosander, thanks to the mediation of the Duchesse d'Orléans, had been able to examine in detail.

At the time of Sophie Charlotte's death, on 15 February 1705, evidently only part of the western extension of the old palace had been completed: internal construction continued on this side until 1706, and only then began on the east side. One striking feature of both Pitzler's and Broebes's view is the absence of the cupola. In his 1704 view, Pitzler still shows the large bay without external staircase. WB

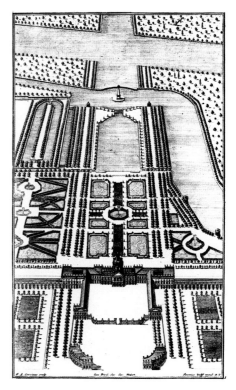

Johann August Corvinus, after a plan by Eosander Göthe (1669–1728): 'Eigentliche Abbildung des Prächtigen Königlichen Lust Schlosses Charlottenburg / eine Meile von Berlin, sambt den darhinden im Walde gelegenen schönen Lustgarten' (True Likeness of the Magnificent Royal Palace of Charlottenburg / One Mile from Berlin, together with the Fine Palace Gardens that Lie in the Forest Beyond)
Etching, c. 1710

Oval Hall on the upper storey after its reconstruction at the beginning of 1960, looking south. The mirror-decoration is based on an inventory description of 1705

24

The Extension of the Palace under King Friedrich I after 1705

Sophie Charlotte died suddenly on 15 February 1705, shortly after arriving in Hanover. Electress Sophie wanted Lietzenburg to be named 'Königinnenburg' ('The Queen's Palace'), but Friedrich I decided on 'Charlottenburg'.

Charlottenburg now became the king's favourite summer residence, and thus the most important building after the Royal Palace. Shortly after the queen's death, the crown prince, writing to his grandmother in Hanover, said that: 'The King goes often to Charlottenburg, in order to accustom himself to taking his regular summer vacation there.' At the end of September 1705, the king decided 'to make Charlottenburg an incomparably beautiful place, in everlasting memory of her late-lamented majesty'. He generally resided at Charlottenburg from April until the second half of October, returning then to the Royal Palace in Berlin. He was therefore able personally to supervise the ongoing improvements to the buildings and grounds.

One scheme of which the king was particularly fond was that for a tower and cupola. His enthusiasm waxed when, in 1707, the Münzturm (more than 100 metres high), which Schlüter had designed for the Royal Palace, was discovered to have inadequate foundations and had to be demolished; in addition, Eosander's plans for a tower over the portal at the Royal Palace got no further than the drawing-board. Interestingly, the tower-scheme, like previous schemes, attracted a tender from a foreign architect. This was the Frenchman Charles Louis Rémy de La Fosse (c. 1666–1726), who was employed between 1706 and 1714 as 'first architect to the electoral court of Hanover'. La Fosse's plans for the palaces at Wilhelmshöhe, Mannheim, and Darmstadt are some of 'the most impressive royal building-projects of the age'. The plan which he drew up in 1706 for Charlottenburg involves some interesting alternative schemes: in contrast to Eosander, he envisaged the cupola room overlooking the courtyard as a projecting pavilion as well, considerably emphasizing the impact of the projection by means of a balustraded balcony resting on double columns. His first design for the cupola, on a low tambour and ending at the level of the ridge of the *corps de logis*, displays clear parallels – even including the crown – with the cupola design for the earliest version of the palace. As an alternative, he offers a tower with an open arcaded storey accommodating bells. La Fosse had also envisaged two large staircases that were to open into the central entrances of the round hall. However, it was Eosander's scheme that was implemented. The hall in this is also round, but set within a square, and it presents a straight frontage on the courtyard side.

The powerful tower, with its attica and arcaded storey, confers a magisterial

Commemorative medal marking the death of Queen Sophie Charlotte on 1 February 1705
Silver, diam. 45 mm
Berlin, 1705
Signed on neckpiece by the Leipzig medallist Rosina Elisabeth Schindel

Friedrich Wilhelm Weidemann (1668–1750)
Friedrich I in Coronation Attire
Oil on canvas, after 1701

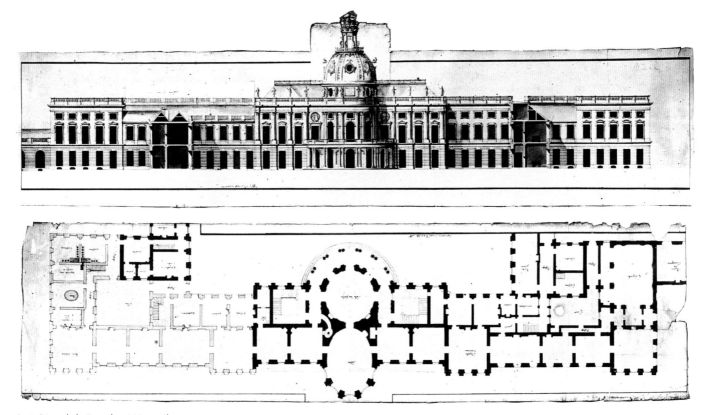

Louis Rémy de la Fosse (c. 1666–1726)
View of front façade and ground plan, with designs
for tower
Wash drawing, c. 1706
Dresden, Landesamt für Denkmalpflege

Johann Böcklin after Eosander Göthe (1669–1728)
View of the courtyard façade after the final extension
by Eosander, c. 1712
Engraving

air not only on the central building, but on the entire site. As in the case of Schlüter's Münzturm and Eosander's planned portal-tower at the Royal Palace, the whole is topped off with a huge gilded, embossed copper statue of Fortuna that serves as a weathervane. The king's penchant for bells was also accommodated at Charlottenburg. Until as late as 1940, three largish bells hung in the cupola, the lucarnes (or dormer windows) serving as sound-holes for these.

However, in July 1708, even before the planned tower was executed (this was done in 1710), the king wrote to Hanover to say 'that everything is changed in Charlottenburg'. The ceiling of the old banqueting-hall in the pavilion on the garden side was substantially raised, and instead of the staircase on pillars that appeared in various guises on the older plans, there was now a French-style unbraced stairway running round the edge of the room – a totally new phenomenon in German palaces of the time. The ceiling painting, by Anthonie de Coxie, depicted Apollo and the Muses, and was intended as homage to the divine company of Muses. The king described the magnificent staircase as 'the finest ornament of the whole house'. Now that large-scale court-ceremonial for foreign envoys was on the Charlottenburg agenda, a *grand escalier* was of particular importance as an allusion to the regal host. The width of the steps was such that they could accommodate a military guard of honour when particularly grand receptions required this.

The increased requirements in terms of court-ceremonial were also taken into account in the great outer courtyard (*avant-cour*) as projected on Eosander's ideal view. The entrance to this was to have been closed off in imposing manner by one-storey, quarter-circle constructions recalling Tessin's design at the royal palace in Stockholm. The military ceremonial enacted by the guards when foreign dignitaries arrived could have taken place at this spot. The pincer-like entrance of the *avant-cour* accentuated the straight line of the approach road, which itself lay at right angles to the major route from the Royal Palace. Construction of this road, which ran through the linden-groves (*die Linden*) and the Tiergarten and resembled the Champs-Elysées, had been set in train as early as 1647 by the Great Elector, to a Dutch design.

The surviving green cast-iron railings, with their gilded decoration and stars of the Order of the Black Eagle, founded by Friedrich I in 1701, were to have marked the boundary between the *avant-cour* and the internal courtyard or *cour d'honneur*.

View onto the staircase designed *c.* 1704 by Eosander Göthe (1669–1728)
Presumed to be the first cantilever stairway in Germany. The cast-iron balustrade was reconstructed from fragments. The ceiling painting by Anthonie de Coxie (after 1650–1720), which depicted *Apollo and the Muses*, has been replaced by a painting of clouds.

The king also planned to have two orangeries built, each 143 metres long and each with their own gardens, on either side of the palace site, but only the western orangery was completed. This had a two-storey, lavishly decorated square

Eosander Göthe (1669–1728)
Chapel in Charlottenburg Palace. View south from the
royal box onto the altar
Ceiling painting by Anthonie Coxie (1650–1720), 1708

View of Great Orangery, looking south-west across the
Orangery garden, with chapel and cupola

The carved and gilded altar, and probably also the
pulpit (c. 1705), are by Charles King (c. 1656–1756),
an Englishman appointed court sculptor in 1703

central pavilion with recessed gallery and a decorative scheme that continued along the entire length of the building. The Orangery was particularly important during the summer months, when the flower containers were planted up and the building was used as a grand banqueting-hall.

The internal decoration of the adjoining palace-rooms, forming a large-scale extension to the original *corps de logis*, began from the west side. The high point came with the consecration of the palace chapel, which took place on 5 December 1706, as part of the wedding festivities for the crown prince. As Eosander wrote, the queen 'wished the place which she dedicated to God to be the most sumptuous compared with everything else in her palace'. The double-aisled span with recessed gallery in the side-aisle was echoed on the Orangery side by a blind arcade with painting designed to create the illusion of space and comprising a rudimentary false gallery. The central source of light, as is to some extent traditional in palace chapels, is a rectangular shaft with superposed skylight. Eosander had adopted a similar approach in the Royal Palace. Taken together with the vaulted ceiling, the Charlottenburg version reminds one of the famous staircase by Nicodemus Tessin the Elder in Drottningholm Palace (near Stockholm). The unusually powerful, sumptuous polychromy of the chapel gives one an idea of how colourful and bold the three other halls in the baroque palace – the two upper rooms at the centre and the magnificent staircase – must have been. These are now decorated in a later cool, classical white, with touches of gilding.

The iconographic scheme in the chapel juxtaposes Old and New Testament themes evoking the virtues of kingship. In his book of engravings *Theatrum Europeum*, Eosander published a picture of the royal box, topped with its great drapery, outsize crown, and Prussian eagle. This rather melodramatic installation is modelled on a similar baldachin, inspired by Tessin the Younger's designs, over the pews of the royal consorts of Sweden in Stockholm Cathedral (Storkyrkan).

Immediately next to the chapel is another famous room, also completed in 1706. This is the 'rare porcelain chamber' of which Eosander published two copper engravings. The carefully chosen theme of the ceiling painting by the Mechelen-born artist Anthonie Coxie (1650–1720), who was also responsible for the paintings in the chapel, underlines the significance of this room: Aurora, the goddess of dawn, in her seven-horsed chariot, chases away Night, clearing the way for the sun-god Apollo, who approaches in his chariot in a blaze of light in the background. Mercury, hovering ahead, heralds the arrival of the life-giving god. Atop the whole scene towers the powerful figure of Saturn, with his scythe, ushering in – as Ovid says – the Golden Age. Witnessing the scene we have not only the four corners of the earth, but also allegories of the four seasons of the year painted on the encircling balustrade. The victory of light over darkness, as depicted here, was much favoured in baroque palaces as a metaphor for glorious kingship.

This great Porcelain Chamber was badly damaged in 1943, and its collection is now made up chiefly of items acquired since the war. Originally, however, it contained over 3,000 pieces of Chinese and Japanese porcelain dating from the second half of the seventeenth century. Eosander converted these into a priceless form of movable wall-decoration. The idea was to overawe the visitor with a feeling both of lavishness – heightened by the multiplicatory effect of the mirrored walls – and of wide-ranging international connections. The Porcelain Chamber in Charlottenburg is one of the last tokens of a porcelain-collecting passion that was once rife in the palaces of Europe. In 1709, on the occasion of the 'meeting of

Eosander Göthe (1669–1728)
Chapel (1704–8) in Charlottenburg Palace, north wall
with royal box

Eosander Göthe (1669–1728)
North wall of the chapel, with royal box
Engraving from Johann Böcklin's *Theatrum
Europaeum*, Part XVI, 1701–3, Frankfurt/Main 1717

Deßein du Chœur dans la Chapelle à Charlottenbourg où
la Maison Royalle est assise pour entendre le sermon.

the three kings' – Frederick of Denmark, August the Strong, and the Prussian king – in Charlottenburg, the room made such an enduring impression on the two guests that they were prompted to imitate it in Rosenborg Palace in Copenhagen and in the Japanese Palace in Dresden.

The Porcelain Chamber was the starting-point for the great enfilade of thirteen royal rooms whose interlinking doors all lay along one axis, so that, when they were all open, it was possible to see 140 metres down through the huge apartments.

One very important craftsman as far as the interior decoration at Charlottenburg was concerned was the English oak-carver Charles King (*c.* 1656–1756), a pupil of the famous woodcarver Grinling Gibbons, who was employed in various English palaces. We have King to thank not only for the pulpit in the palace chapel and the elaborately carved oak doors in the halls, but also for the carving of the highly architectural panelling in the Grande Galerie. Because it served as a portrait gallery of the Hohenzollern dynasty, this hall – the most consistently 'English' in feel – was also known as the Ahnengalerie or Ancestors' Gallery. In the centre, over the fireplace, hangs a full-length portrait of Friedrich I in coronation attire. This was executed by the court painter Friedrich Wilhelm Weidemann (1668–1750). The paintings in the mirror niches illustrate episodes from Fénélon's *Les Aventures de Télémaque*, the 'Fürstenspiegel' (handbook for princes) published in 1699. The room was evidently unfinished at the time of the death of the king in 1713, and this is undoubtedly why the projected painting of the barrel vaulting was never done.

At about the same time as the Great Oak Gallery was constructed, a Petite Galerie came into being in the west wing, adjoining Sophie Charlotte's Second Apartment. This too was decorated with English-style oakwood panelling. The room later came to be known as the 'Japanese' or 'Porcelain' Gallery, when, after 1740, Friedrich II brought the six carved and gilded sets of shelving bearing numerous pieces of porcelain from the collection of Friedrich III in the Oranienburg (north of Berlin), to Charlottenburg.

The change in style which took place over these few years of construction at Charlottenburg emerges particularly clearly if one compares the grandiose stucco ceilings produced around 1697–8 with the stucco-less ceiling painting in the small, intimate apartments on the courtyard side – Sophie Charlotte's Second Apartment and the Mecklenburg Rooms – as executed under the direction of Eosander after 1702. This meticulous, detailed painting, comprising grotesques and arabesques in the manner of Jean Bérain, is most often executed on a white ground, less often against a monochrome coloured backing. The design consists of a filigree edging with motifs at the corners and half-way along, and a central painting that sets the iconographical theme for the ceiling. WB

Porcelain Chamber
Ceiling painting by Anthonie Coxie (1650–1720):
*Aurora, Goddess of Dawn, Drives away the Forces
of Darkness,* 1706; restored early 1970
The process of refurnishing the room with Chinese
porcelain dating from about 1700 was completed in
1993.

Green Chamber in the king's suite
According to the inventory of 1770, this room was lined with green satinade and served as Friedrich I's study. The French mirror was part of the room's original furnishings.
Set of porcelain vases: Chinese Imari, c. 1700

Friedrich Wilhelm Weidemann (attributed to)
Conclusion of the Alliance of the Three Kings Frederick August II of Poland, Friedrich I, King in Prussia, and Frederick IV of Denmark, against Charles XII of Sweden, 12 June 1709 in Charlottenburg Palace, 1709
Oil on canvas, 253 x 195 cm
Lent by the Freunde der Preußischen Schlösser und Gärten

Panelled Corner-Room
Directly adjoining the Oak Gallery to the east, this oak-panelled room is the counterpart to the Porcelain Chamber at the opposite end of the garden tract. The cartouche with intertwined 'Fridericus Rex' monogram in the arched panel over the fireplace evokes Friedrich I, who used to use this room as a 'dining-chamber'

Red Chamber in the king's suite
The feature that gave this room its name was the red damask wall-covering with rich gold ornamental braiding. The room is now often called the 'Red-Braid Room'. The decoration that originally adorned the ceiling (now white) did not survive.

Japanese Gallery – also known as the Porcelain Gallery – with the shelving from Friedrich III's porcelain room in Oranienburg Palace, c. 1695 Chinese blue-and-white items and Japanese Imari *jardinières c.* 1700

Ceiling of bedroom in the Mecklenburg Apartment In the centre is an *Allegory of Night*: Putti support the baldachin extending to the ceiling and the drapery over the mirror (not visible here).

The Baroque Garden

he area of land north of the village of Lütze, within the broad curve of the River Spree, which was selected for the construction of the palace of Lützenburg or Lietzenburg, was described as 'completely overgrown' in the seventeenth century. The choice of the site was determined not just by the space it afforded, but, most importantly, by the proximity of the River Spree. Not only was this situation ideal in terms of the irrigation of the grounds and the laying of dikes, lakes, and waterworks; it also offered ideal connections by boat to Berlin and the other palaces. The most important electoral palaces were either located on the Spree or the Havel, or, where this was not possible, were linked to the rivers by canals. Friedrich III was very keen on pleasure craft.

As a child, Sophie Charlotte had been familiar not only with the gardens created by her mother at home in Iburg and Osnabrück, but also with the Hortus Palatinus, the most important German garden of the Renaissance period, which was part of the palace at Heidelberg, the home of her grandfather Friedrich V of the Palatinate. Besides this, in 1679 she accompanied her mother to France, where she visited the gardens in Fontainebleau, Saint-Cloud, and Versailles. The combined memory of all these places lived on in the garden-schemes at Herrenhausen and Lietzenburg, which were begun more or less simultaneously. Between 1696 and 1714, Electress Sophie commissioned Martin Charbonnier to extend the Great Gardens at Herrenhausen (near Hanover) by 182 acres, and she herself became personally deeply involved in the creation of the most important baroque garden in Germany. At Herrenhausen, the design was based on established Dutch and French models and was more conventional and probably also deliberately more traditional. In Lietzenburg, in contrast, the young electress used the rare opportunity of a completely fresh start in order to work to the latest French guide-lines. Like other major royals of the day, she had sought advice, through her cousin the Duchesse d'Orléans, from the most famous gardener of the time: André Le Nôtre, 'jardinier de Louis XIV' (1613–1700). Le Nôtre, himself fully occupied, dispatched his pupil Siméon Godeau to Lietzenburg. But Sophie Charlotte sought reassurance and asked that Godeau's plans be checked by Le Nôtre himself. Godeau's first scheme, which survived until 1945, envisaged the whole garden being laid out crosswise in relation to the palace, offering three lines of sight: one running west (in the direction of Spandau Castle), one running north (in the direction of Tegel Palace), and one running north-east (in the direction of Schönhausen). The garden was even meant to extend over the Spree, in a north-westerly direction. When it came to the actual execution, however, only the avenue-like sight-lines remained. In the first design to be carried out, work

Charlottenburg Palace and palace grounds, restored in baroque style after 1950. Hidden in the trees is the cupola of the Belvedere
Photo: 1990

was restricted to the terrain naturally offered by the Spree, which meant a vertical orientation was inevitable. About 900 metres north of the palace, Godeau cut a dike that ran from the Spree towards the palace and opened into a small artificial lake. On Eosander's bird's-eye view of the palace, the lake, 2 metres in depth, not only provided a mooring-point for the royal yachts; it was also meant to stand out in its own right as a water feature in the overall scheme of the garden, an effect achieved through the vertical lines of four huge water-jets reminiscent of Le Nôtre's Parterre d'Eau at Versailles. Next to the lake lay a raised *parterre* about 250 metres long and 100 metres wide. This was set out, mirror-style, as *broderie* or 'embroidery', made up of flower-beds (*plate-bandes*), strips of light-coloured sand, sections of lawn (*massifs*), and areas of light-coloured sand and red gravel artistically encircled by dwarf box-trees. Wide strips of lawn

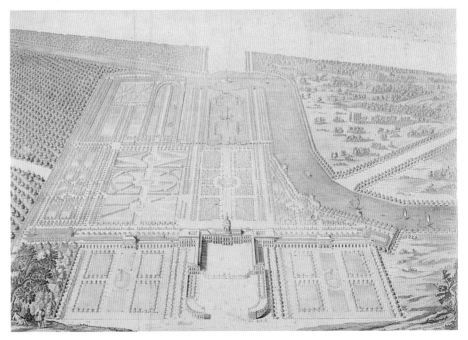

Martin Engelbrecht (1684–1756) after Eosander Göthe (1669–1728)
Bird's-eye view of the palace site, 1708–10
Engraving

(*allées vertes*) criss-crossed the whole *parterre*, and at the point where they converged there was to have been a huge fountain.

Dézallier d'Argenvilles' garden handbook *La Théorie et pratique du jardinage*, first published in 1709, uses the term 'parterre de broderie mêlée des massifs de gazon' to describe this kind of arrangement of formal beds. Given the amount of flat decoration, the various vertical lines in the design were of considerable importance. According to Pitzler's drawing of 1704, these were at first provided by obelisks of lattice-work painted green, white, and yellow, statues 'of lead, gilded' – representing figures from Roman mythology – and large vases. Recent research has rightly identified this accumulation of movable decorative items as the only example of recourse to older Dutch traditions at Lietzenburg. In his final plan Eosander Göthe replaced them with cone-shaped yew-trees, in line with the newer French taste.

If one looks out over this central section of the garden from the palace, the importance of this great medial, northward axis is also evident from the fact that it is the only area systematically flanked by rows of linden trees, thus linking flower-beds, the palace lake, and even the line of sight beyond the Spree. Given the great depth of the perspective, Godeau inserted an additional *point de vue* or focus, aligned with the water-jet in the flower-garden fountain. This took the form of an obelisk, set on an artificial island in the Spree and towering above all the other features.

Along the façade of the palace ran a horizontal terrace, five steps high. It was bounded by a wall and flower-bed, punctuated by a staircase and side-ramps. This dividing-line was accentuated by means of a compact row of sandstone figures, vases, and cone-shaped orange-trees. On the short sides of the palace, along the walls of the Orangeries (of which only one was executed), there ran narrow pergolas of green-painted, arched lattice-work (*berceau de treillage*). By means of them, the enfilade extended, as it were, into the garden, in the same way that Eosander had achieved at Monbijou Palace. At both ends, the pergolas led into largish *berceaux carrés*, with green-lawned quadrangles. The larger *carré* (58 metres long) at the western end, with its double arcades, corner pavilions, and encircling rooftop balustrade, was of much tighter architectural design. It was in the eastern *carré*, which fronted onto the Spree, that Sophie Charlotte,

Paul Decker the Younger (1685–1742)
View of garden front with terrace, 1705–6
Nuremberg, Germanisches Nationalmuseum

one summer night in 1702, staged the musical one-act play *I Trionfi di Parnasso*, probably composed by herself.

According to d'Argenvilles, a very important component of a baroque garden was the hornbeam hedging (*bosquet*), cut like walls. At Lietzenburg this was about 2 metres tall. One could never have enough of this kind of hedging, since it afforded shade from the summer heat for those wanting a quiet *tête-à-tête*. Compared with the *parterre*, which was flooded with light, and in which one strolled with the aim of being seen, the hedging was both functionally and structurally quite different in purpose. Godeau had chosen the area west of the *parterre* for the *bosquets*, and had created three sections of equal size. A striking feature of the first *bosquet* is the northwardly displaced star-shaped system of paths. The sight-line that radiates diagonally – that is to say, westwards – from the *corps de logis*, in the direction of Spandau, can clearly be seen here. Another, north–south line cuts through all the *bosquets*, right to the end of the garden, each intersecting the three centres (*salles*), with their fountains, on alternating plans.   WB

37

The New Wing
in Frederick the Great's
Time

hen Friedrich der Große (Frederick the Great, 1712–1786) assumed power in May 1740, following the death of his father, Friedrich Wilhelm I, the 'Soldier King', he had already been living for four years in the crown prince's residence at Rheinsberg, about 80 kilometres north of Berlin. Here, on the edges of Grinerick lake, in the palace redesigned and arranged to his specifications by Georg Wenceslaus von Knobelsdorff (1699–1753), Friedrich was able to devote himself entirely to his philosophical and musical passions. Rheinsberg was his refuge from, and counter to, the soldierly world of his father, dominated by the notions of obedience and duty. Here, in an intimate court-circle that included artists such as Knobelsdorff and Antoine Pesne (1683–1757), the crown prince spent happy times engaged in music, dancing, and games.

The paradigm for this kind of court life, with its characteristic mix of fiction and reality, was the imaginary world of Antoine Watteau (1684–1721). As crown prince, Friedrich had already begun to collect paintings by this artist, and by his pupils Nicolas Lancret (1690–1745) and Jean-Baptiste Pater (1695–1736), as decoration for his apartments and palaces. In this way, a unique collection came into being, ultimately comprising thirteen paintings by Watteau, twenty-six by Lancret, and thirty-seven by Pater. It was only in the mid-1750s that the king's taste began to veer towards the Italian and Dutch schools, as a result of the influence of his adviser Duke Algarotti. The dream-world of Watteau-style *fêtes galantes* embodied the ideal existence to which the young Friedrich aspired. This was such a determining influence during his period as crown prince, that in a work published at a later date, Baron von Bielefeldt, himself a member of the Rheinsberg court-circle, could compare life at Rheinsberg to a painting by Watteau, in contrast with the prosaic life at Potsdam, which he likened to a painting in the style of Rembrandt.

Friedrich's Rheinsberg days had a decisive influence on his later architectural enterprises. This is evident not only in the evolution of the palace and grounds of Sanssouci (1747), but also in the New Wing at Charlottenburg. Construction of the latter as a future residence was begun immediately after Friedrich's accession.

Georg Wenceslaus von Knobelsdorff, Friedrich's friend and artistic mentor in the early years, seems to have begun the plans for the new residence whilst still in Rheinsberg. What turned the scales in favour of Charlottenburg is uncertain. Knobelsdorff produced a design – of which only the ground-plan has come down to us – for a great royal palace on Unter den Linden in Berlin, more or less on the site of the later palace for Prince Heinrich (now Humboldt University), and it is clear from this that at that stage the king was planning something grander.

Antoine Pesne (1683–1757)
King Friedrich Wilhelm I (1688–1740) Commands the Armed Forces at the Siege of Stralsund (1715)
Oil on canvas, 1729

Georg Wenceslaus von Knobelsdorff (1699–1753)
Crown Prince Friedrich (II)
Pastel, c. 1735

Antoine Pesne (1683–1757)
Frederick the Great as a child, with his favourite sister,
Wilhelmine (1709–58), later Margravine of Bayreuth
Oil on canvas, 1714

The 'Forum Fridericianum', as it was known – a U-shaped structure with a main courtyard enclosed by a colonnade and two end-buildings – would not only have rivalled Friedrich I's royal palace; it would also have had a lasting influence on the later architectural development of Berlin.

Against this background, the choice of Charlottenburg appears to have been much the more modest solution. Perhaps a certain degree of deference in regard to his grandmother, the renowned Sophie Charlotte, also played a role here – although Friedrich had made no secret of his reservations about the building programme pursued by her consort, Friedrich I. There may also have been financial reasons for opting for construction at Charlottenburg – combined with a certain pique *vis-à-vis* his father, because, when the latter had assumed power in 1713, the construction of Charlottenburg had had to be abruptly broken off. Most of the artists and craftsmen had been unable to find any other work, and so had left Prussia. The cessation of the building-works meant that the Orangery planned for the eastern end, as a match to the one already completed in the west, was never built. Friedrich had thus found a site that was large enough for a royal residence and at the same time allowed him to complete the structure begun by his grandparents.

Knobelsdorff, now appointed Surveyor-General of Royal Palaces and Parks, adhered precisely to the existing ground-plans for the Orangery but added an extra storey. Externally, the New Wing was plain. The only extra emphasis was provided by the central projection, with its strong, jutting orders at ground level, its pilaster-divisions on the first floor, its robust entablature, and a concluding series of vases that pick up the vertical stress. In terms of architectural style, the long, rather cool building reflected a formal ideal shaped by English Palladianism.

In contrast, but by no means in conflict, with this approach, was an internal wealth of decoration. As will be shown, this aspect presented patron and architect with particular problems, given the task of providing the appropriate imposing setting for a royal residence.

View of New Wing by Wenceslaus von Knobelsdorff (1699–1753), looking south-west across the 'ducal' garden

The Grounds

At the same time as the New Wing was constructed, the palace grounds were restored and rearranged. Under Friedrich Wilhelm I, only the most basic maintenance-work had been undertaken. Thus, in 1742, 6,000 'fine young straight lindens' were purchased from Holland. A thousand of these went to Potsdam. In 1744, on Friedrich's orders, 3,000 linden trees were bought for the pleasure-gardens at Charlottenburg, along with a quantity of fruit-trees for the kitchen-gardens.

In addition, Friedrich adorned the park with twenty-four busts of the Julian emperors and their consorts. These 'had previously lain locked up and hidden', having, according to tradition, been created for the elector by the sculptor Kaspar Günther. They were now positioned on herms in a line along the garden façade. At either end of the latter stood the statues of the Great Elector by François Dusart and of Elector Friedrich I by Gabriel Grupello. Eleven sets of children's figures were also positioned in front of the New Wing, probably alternating with the herms. The garden itself was provided with a wealth of sculptural decoration, in the form of forty-nine *putti*.

The Construction Work and the Interior Decoration

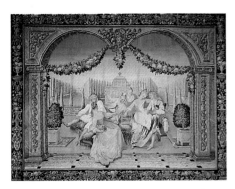

Audience Chamber in Sophie Charlotte's First Apartment. The tapestry by the Berlin workshop of Charles Vigne (d. 1751) depicts a *scène galante* with two young lovers seated on a bench (motifs to designs by Lancret and Watteau). Monbijou Palace, the home of Frederick the Great's mother, Sophie Dorothea (1687–1757) is pictured in the background.

Work at Charlottenburg began in summer 1740, the king having moved there immediately after his accession to the throne. As early as 5 July 1740, the *Spenersche Zeitung* reported that 'since the necessary building materials are already available, an immediate start [is to be made] on the extension of the palace of Charlottenburg, where a New Wing is to be built'. Two other buildings – a royal stable and an Orangery – were already complete, and the intention was to get to a similar stage with the New Wing by the end of the year. However, the king was unable to follow the work at close quarters: in the winter of 1741 he set off to conquer Silesia. None the less, he took an avid interest in the progress of construction at Charlottenburg.

No report, however detailed, was ever enough for him: this kind of news offered him respite from his duties. In May 1742 he wrote with annoyance to Jordan, his close friend in Berlin: 'I have received a letter from Knobelsdorff. I am satisfied with it, but everything in it is too dry; there is no detail. I would like the description of every portion of column in Charlottenburg to take up four sides of quarto. That would please me.' In the same month, Jordan is asked to get 'that lump Knobelsdorff' to let him know how the building-works in Charlottenburg, in his gardens, and at the Berlin opera are getting on. 'I'm like a child about them; they're my dolls, my playthings.'

On 15 June 1742, peace was concluded. The king instructed Jordan to press Knobelsdorff to complete the work at Charlottenburg, because, he said, he intended to spend a good deal of his time there. On 12 July the king finally arrived at the palace, where he was welcomed by his friends and celebrated as an architectural patron in a series of laudatory verses by Voltaire, whom the king would have liked to have in his company. And yet at this stage, only the external construction, the White Hall, and a few other rooms in his apartments were complete. In 1743 a huge banquet was given in the White Hall. The *Spenersche Zeitung* of 29 August of that year reported that the king had held 'a magnificent feast in the newly constructed wing of the palace'. The internal work extended over several more years. The Golden Gallery was not inaugurated until October 1746. This was the largest and finest room in the new residence, and one of the most magnificent examples of Frederican interior decoration. On that occasion the *Spenersche Zeitung* talked of the first festivity to have taken place, on 7 October 1746, 'in the magnificent newly constructed gallery of the palace'.

Whilst the New Wing was being constructed, a number of rooms in the old palace were newly painted or had their walls relined with damask. But this was more upkeep than alteration – except in the case of two rooms formerly belonging to Sophie Charlotte on the ground floor west of the Oval Hall, on the garden side of the building. These were fitted out with six tapestries by the Berlin manufactory of Charles Vigne. The tapestries – still remarkably well preserved – were

Friederike Meinert (exhibited at Berlin Academy 1836–48)
Green Chamber with Frederican panelling by Christian Friedrich Glume (1714–52)
Watercolour, 1843

made in 1740 and depicted courting couples and *commedia dell'arte* figures executed as free renderings of Watteau-style images.

More practical purposes probably lay behind the rearrangement, in 1743, of two rooms located to the east of the upper Oval Hall. Both these rooms – destroyed in the last war – were lined with light green/white panelling and were decorated with carved silvered or gilded ornamentation. The work was carried out by the sculptor Friedrich Christian Glume (1714–1752), who had previously worked at Rheinsberg. The old-fashioned, ponderous, and rather clumsy forms still displayed the modest artistic standards of Friedrich Wilhelm I's day. These two rooms illustrate the problems and difficulties that arose in the course of the interior decoration of the New Wing. Friedrich did indeed intend to make his residence as imposing as possible, but the sort of artistic talents needed for this were just not available. The haemorrhage of craftsman and decorators that had taken place at the time of Friedrich Wilhelm I's accession was now making itself felt. When he assumed power, the king therefore found himself obliged to place an appeal in various newspapers, calling on all artists outside the country to come to Prussia.

One of the sculptors who responded to this appeal was Johann August Nahl the Elder (1710–1781), probably the most renowned of the Frederican ornamental sculptors. The artistically no less talented brothers Johann Michael Hoppenhaupt (known as 'the Elder', 1709–1755) and Johann Christian Hoppenhaupt (known as 'the Younger', d. *c.* 1780), whose profession was likewise sculpture and ornamental carving, also entered the service of the Prussian king at this time. To begin with, however, the king had to have recourse to such talents as were available at home, and one of the results of this is that in the apartments of the New Wing, there is a juxtaposition of very high-quality and relatively modest decoration. Other variations in style and quality stemmed from the fact that in Charlottenburg, as in later decorative projects, Friedrich had the habit of sharing the tasks out between several decorators, who were allowed to pursue their own stylistic paths within a single overall scheme.

Friedrich probably sometimes provided his own designs for interior decoration. According to Manger's *Baugeschichte von Potsdam*, during the first forty years of his reign, the king 'himself devised and designed the exterior of the palaces that were to be built – and also the decoration and furnishing in the internal apartments of those buildings especially associated with him; in latter years, he was not so particular in this regard'.

If one looks at Friedrich's famous sketches for his summer residence at Sanssouci, or at his many drawings of mansion-house façades in Potsdam, one can probably safely say that what he gave was no more than a rough outline. Given this way of working, it was inevitable that certain stylistic discrepancies – for example, between wall and ceiling decoration – should arise. And yet Frederican interior decoration comes across as relatively unified stylistically speaking. This is probably due in no small part to the Surveyor-General of Palaces, Georg Wenceslaus von Knobelsdorff, Friedrich's friend and artistic mentor in the early years. Himself a highly talented and extraordinarily skilled designer of interior decoration, Knobelsdorff appears to have had not only a corrective, but also a generally stimulating and inspirational influence.

The Apartments of Queen Elisabeth Christine

The first suite of rooms to be completed in the New Wing was the apartment of Frederick the Great's consort, Elisabeth Christine of Braunschweig-Bevern (1715–1797). The king's relations with his spouse were already troubled at that time, and the apartments were probably therefore created more for reasons of etiquette than for any practical purpose. At any rate, Elisabeth Christine never occupied them.

Since the king laid claim to the whole of the first-floor *piano nobile* west of the central staircase, Elisabeth Christine had to content herself with the ground-floor accommodation, which had lower ceilings. The decoration of these apartments remained within relatively modest limits. Completed in 1742, they comprised a total of seven rooms – two more than Elisabeth Christine had occupied at Rheinsberg. They underwent an almost complete overhaul soon after 1800, at the time of Friedrich Wilhelm III, so that only the fireplaces from the Antechamber, the Parade Chamber and the Bedchamber, and the painted decorations from the Japanese Chamber remain to give us an idea of the original state of these rooms. There were no plans, as in Friedrich's apartments, for ceiling paintings in any of these rooms. Another striking feature is the absence of silvered decoration, much loved by Friedrich. The decoration and ornament seems to have been gilded, as in the crown princess's apartments at Rheinsberg.

From the Hall, the visitor first entered a wood-panelled Antechamber with gilded decoration, and from there the queen's Audience Chamber. As mentioned by Daun in his report of 1760 about the damage caused by the Cossacks and Austrians, this room was done out 'in silk'. The name of this largely unknown pupil of Pesne is also associated with the wall-paintings in the antechamber of Friedrich's apartments. These survived until the war, and more will be said about them later. As in those apartments, one should here imagine an illusionistic landscape in oils, populated with courtly ladies and gentlemen.

After the Audience Chamber came the Japanese Chamber, which survives today. The panelling here is painted with bizarre jutting, filigree-like rococo structures on which Chinese figures lounge, play musical instruments, or hunt. The painting, executed mainly in green tones on a white ground, accentuated here and there with brightly coloured flowers, imitates porcelain and must once have made a much more vivid impression than it does today in its sometimes greatly faded state. Wilhelm Höder (d. *c.* 1761) specialized in Chinese grotesque painting, and further examples of his work may be seen in the guest-rooms at Sanssouci. The Charlottenburg paintings were not discovered until 1945, under the charred remains of the wall-covering applied over them at the end of the eighteenth century. Having been carefully restored during the last few years, they have recently returned to their original positions.

Passing through a room lined with red-striped satin, one finally reached the panelled royal Bedchamber, the decoration of which is markedly more lavish than that of the other rooms. This chamber also contained the large, beautifully proportioned, vase-adorned four-poster bed known to us from a sketch by Knobelsdorff. Completing this suite were: two further, more simply decorated rooms

Antoine Pesne (1683–1757)
Queen Elisabeth Christine (1715–97), Consort of Frederick the Great
Oil on canvas, *c.* 1740

New Wing, apartment of Queen Elisabeth Christine (1715–97), consort of Frederick the Great, 'Japanese Room', with grotesque painting by Friedrich Wilhelm Höder (d. c. 1761)
The showpiece-table (c. 1745), with its powerful, almost baroque vocabulary of forms, constitutes one of the finest creations of Frederican furniture-making

to the west; the Parade Chamber, which had a painted satin wall-covering; and a simple Antechamber leading directly into the old palace.

Frederick the Great's First Apartment

The royal apartment, the decoration of which was completed in the mid-1740s, was situated on the upper floor of the New Wing and is known as the First Apartment, to distinguish it from the Second Apartment that was arranged at a later date at the eastern end of the building. It comprised eight rooms to the front of the building, and five facing the garden. As a result of the alterations carried out under Frederick the Great's successors, only three rooms on the garden side have survived: the Silver Antechamber, the Library, and Friedrich's Study. They were the most private of all the rooms in the apartment and were therefore lavishly decorated. From the point of view both of their colour and of the nature of the materials used, they conveyed an impression of great diversity.

Approaching Friedrich's apartments from the main staircase, one first entered a room which, like the 'silk-lined chamber' in Elisabeth's apartments, was painted with illusionistic scenes. The painting, hidden under late eight-eenth-century panelling, was discovered and exposed only a short time before its ultimate destruction in the Second World War. Executed in oil on dry plaster, it must have made an astonishing impression on any visitor to the room, who suddenly found himself transported to a setting of courtly festivity and carnival. On all three sides, the room, as it were, extended into a terrace-like structure supported on slender pillars. This offered an immediate view onto high-cut hedges, and behind these, already swathed in atmospheric mist, there appeared the tops of high trees. On the terrace, painted almost life-size, a company of festively attired courtly guests was gathered. As in Watteau's *fêtes galantes* – whose inspiration here is unmistakable – the gentlemen and ladies moved and posed as on a stage, as both spectators and actors. The group as a whole remained anonymous; any allusion to specific individuals living at Friedrich's court was not discernible.

The name of the artist who painted these scenes is unknown. The decorative style of the flower-crowned gilded parapets and railings may indicate the hand of Friedrich Wilhelm Höder. Whoever the creator of the paintings was, the skilled ease of his brushwork and the delicacy of his palette indicate close proximity to Antoine Pesne, and he should probably be sought in the latter's circle.

The walls of the next room were decorated with light-coloured marbling, the panels being filled with gilded reliefs depicting scenes from Ovid's *Metamorphoses* and musical symbols. Such images were favourites in other Frederican music rooms, one example being the concert room at Sanssouci, decorated in 1746. The ceiling painting, by Antoine Pesne, was co-ordinated with the themes on the walls: it depicted Apollo and the Muses delicately incorporated into a bright sky filled with billowing clouds.

Connecting with the Marbled Chamber on the western side was the room known as the Yellow Drap d'Argent Chamber. This too was altered under Friedrich Wilhelm II. The only part of the extremely elegant decoration to survive until the Second World War was the ceiling painting by Antoine Pesne, depicting Venus and Cupid.

The next room, the Wood-Panelled Chamber, with its gilded decoration on a white ground, was also substantially altered at the end of the eighteenth century. Only one surviving sketch – probably by the renowned decorative sculptor Johann August Nahl the Elder (1710–1781) – remains to give us an idea of the original state of the room. Given the richness of its ornamental embellishments, it must have been one of the finest examples of decoration in the Frederican apartments.

New Wing, Silver Antechamber (looking east)
Early Frederican interior decoration by Johann August Nahl (1710–81)

Antoine Pesne (1683–1757)
Countess Sophie Marie von Voß (1729–1814) in Hunting Attire
In 1744, at only 15 years of age, Sophie became lady-in-waiting to Sophie Dorothea, consort of Friedrich Wilhelm I. In old age she became Mistress of the Royal Household under Queen Luise (1776–1810). This portrait is one of Pesne's finest works.
Oil on canvas, c. 1746

Antoine Pesne (1683–1757)
Baroness Eleonore von Keyserlingk (1720–55), maid of honour to Queen Elisabeth Christine, consort of Friedrich II
Oil on canvas, c. 1745

To the west, there then followed the Dining Room, a white-panelled room with gilded decoration. Adjoining this was a Silver and Chenille Chamber, which also fell victim to redecoration under Friedrich Wilhelm II. The wall-covering was of silver brocade (*drap d'argent*) with bands of chenille, surrounded by a silvered edging. The curtains and upholstery were of red satin backed with white taffeta. The ceiling painting, depicting Diana and Endymion, was by Harper, a pupil of Pesne's, and was dated 1742.

The walls of the next room, the Yellow Satin Room, were covered with yellow satin sectioned off with rich braiding. Over the doors there were floral motifs by Augustin Dubuisson, Pesne's brother-in-law. The ceiling was decorated with a picture by Pesne representing Iris, the winged messenger of the gods, conveying divine messages to mortals. The lost ceiling painting, with its contrasts of atmosphere, must have been of great lyrical quality.

Since the old panelled window-frames, the plinth panels, and the door, with its silver decoration on white ground, had survived the alterations carried out under Friedrich Wilhelm II, during the post-war period the room was furnished with items from the Frederican inventory. Notable pieces here are the famous full-length portrait of the dancer Barberina, which formerly hung in Friedrich's study in the Royal Palace, the portrait of the dancer Cochois from the concert room in the Stadtschloß in Potsdam, and, last but not least, the famous 1735 pastel of Friedrich as crown prince by Georg Wenceslaus von Knobelsdorff.

Fragments of the old Frederican decoration – the gilt door-surround, for example, and the painted *putti* in the *sopraporte* – are also preserved in the adjoining Antechamber, which is lined with blue satinette. Some of Antoine Pesne's major portraits of ladies-in-waiting may be viewed here, including those of Duchess Voß and Eleonore Baroness Keyserlinck, as well as Elisabeth Dorothea Juliane Baroness Buddenbrock, who, as lady-in-waiting to Elisabeth Christine in Rheinsberg, was a much-fêted beauty.

The king's private rooms, partly reconstructed after the war and including the Silver Antechamber and the Library, contain some of the most lavish and artistically most important interior decoration in the Frederican apartments. The ornamental detail is often highly creative. The meticulously evoked, exuberant rococo foliage at the base of the wall panels in the Silver Antechamber is one of the finest examples of creative work done in the early phase of Frederican interior decoration. Its author was probably Johann August Nahl the Elder, who was also responsible for the elegant ceiling decoration. Overall, the room can now give us only an inadequate impression of its original subtle colouring.

In our mind's eye, we have to add sumptuous curtains of lilac-coloured (*gris de lin*) satin lined with white taffeta and decorated with a rich silver braid. The incoming light was thus slightly refracted, lending the white ground of the silver decoration a violet shimmer of Watteau-like delicacy. The sort of expenditure in which Friedrich sometimes indulged in furnishing his apartment is evident not least from the fact that the console-table that used to stand between the windows was made out of solid silver (it has not survived).

The walls of the Library, decorated in a range of green tones and resembling a gallery, were panelled. Against the chimney wall stood a number of plain, cedarwood bookcases. These now accommodate the books from Friedrich's library in the Stadtschloß in Potsdam, which has since disappeared.

In Friedrich's time, the robust stucco consoles – probably designed by Nahl – supported antique busts from the collection of Cardinal Polignac (1661–1742),

Antoine Pesne (1683–1757)
La Barberina
This life-sized painting of the
Italian dancer Barbara
Campanini (1724–99), who
charmed audiences in Berlin
from 1744 to 1748, was
probably executed especially
for Friedrich II's study in the
Royal Palace, designed by
Nahl in 1745.
Oil on canvas, *c.* 1745

which Friedrich had purchased in 1743. These were donated to the Staatliche Museen in the nineteenth century, being replaced with plaster casts. The original brightness of the room has been diminished by the absence of the two ceiling paintings by Antoine Pesne, which were destroyed during the war. The eastern section portrayed Minerva as guardian of the arts and sciences, enthroned on a cloud and surrounded by *putti*. The right-hand section depicted an allegory, also embodied in female form, of poetry and music. Pesne had already produced a version of this latter theme on the ceiling of Friedrich's library at Rheinsberg.

A particularly welcome stroke of good fortune is the preservation, in this room, of one of the original items of furniture from the library, in the form of a silvered console-table. This piece of work, probably executed by Johann Michael Hoppenhaupt the Elder, is one of the finest examples of a console-table to be found in any

New Wing, the Library in Frederick the Great's First Apartment viewed from the east

of the Frederican palaces and thus gives one an idea of the high standard of furniture-making in this early phase of Frederican interior decoration.

In the display case mounted onto the table's modern-day marble top are eight of Frederick the Great's famous snuff-boxes. The king had a particular penchant for such items, made of semi-precious stones and decorated with diamonds, turquoises, rubies, and emeralds, and he is said to have designed some of them himself. He often presented them as gifts, as a mark of his appreciation or as official thanks to particular individuals.

The wall decoration in Friedrich's small, almost square Study consists of comparatively narrow panels with rococo designs set symmetrically in the middle of the upper and lower edging. The panels are divided off by pilasters filled with chains of flowers. The influence of the older-style Rheinsberg wall-decoration is

New Wing, Friedrich II's study (looking west)
The precious, richly inlaid, fire-gilt clock was designed by Jean-Pierre Latz (c. 1691–1754), c. 1740
'Nahl' chandelier, bronze, fire-gilt, c. 1740–5

Snuff-box
Moss agate, brilliants, gold
Unmarked
Berlin, 1767–71
The decoration on the lid is after François Boucher
(1703–70): Aurora, whose chariot is driven by a *putto,*
dispatches Cupid to the sleeping Cephalus.
Lent by the House of Hohenzollern

Snuff-box with portrait of Friedrich II
Miniature by Johann Harper (1688–1746)
Gold, brilliants, enamel, ivory, glass
Unmarked
Berlin, 1745
This box was presented by Frederick the Great to
Field-Marshal Duke Leopold von Anhalt-Dessau
(1676–1747) as a military decoration following the
'old Dessauer's' defeat of the Saxons and Austrians
at Kesselsdorf on 15 December 1745.

Snuff-box
Red-brown jasper, gold, brilliants
Unmarked
Berlin, *c.* 1765
Lent by the House of Hohenzollern

still detectable in the regular, rather monotonous rhythm of this series of panels. A particularly striking item of furniture in this room is the sumptuous grandfather clock, decorated with hot-gilt bronze fittings. It bears the name of Jean-Pierre Latz (*c.* 1691–1754) and the date 1745. Friedrich seems to have thought very highly of the work of this renowned Parisian cabinet-maker: several examples of these magnificent clocks were to be found in his palaces.

The White Hall and the Golden Gallery

Frederick the Great's decision to install his new residence not in the main building's *corps de logis* but in a side structure originally designed as an orangery

reveals a characteristic trait. Most of his palace-buildings – with the exception of the southern façade of Sanssouci, dominated by its powerful caryatids – have rather plain architectural exteriors. The interiors, on the other hand, were quite sumptuous. So were the furnishings, the rarity and opulence of which it is now hard to imagine.

This contrast between interior and exterior is also observable in the New Wing. The external structure was plain, and rows of linden trees were planted on both sides, right up to the central projection, so that the building as a whole was not visible either from the front or from the garden. Entering through the main entrance in the middle, the visitor found himself in a spacious vestibule with walls of grey imitation marble. The floor was laid with red and white Swedish tiles. From here, he had access to an imposing staircase, sectioned off with

Snuff-box
Gold, enamel, brilliants
Unmarked
Berlin, *c.* 1765–70
The enamel ground is decorated with a mythological scene in *grisaille*: Diana and her companions bathing.
Lent by the House of Hohenzollern

double pilasters. Here too the walls were of grey imitation marble. The ceiling painting was by Antoine Pesne and depicted Prometheus bringing fire to mankind – a theme not without some allusion to the young king.

At the top of the staircase to the west lay the king's main apartments, which have already been described. To the east, two great rooms opened out: the White Hall and the Golden Gallery. The walls of the White Hall, sectioned off with white double pilasters, were originally clad in pink imitation marble. In the course of the nineteenth century, this had faded to white. The ceiling painting, depicting the wedding of Peleus and Thetis, was also by Antoine Pesne. It contained an indirect allusion to the young king's regnal virtues, in that the bride and bridegroom were the parents of the Greek hero Achilles. The model for this room, which was used sometimes as a banqueting-hall and sometimes as a throne room, was the concert-hall at Rheinsberg. The latter's walls were decorated in the same way, and its ceiling painting was also by Antoine Pesne. The grotesque *capricci* of the four seasons, applied freely to the wall-space over the doors, are also modelled on Rheinsberg. With their great debt to Watteau-style decorative art, they constitute some of the finest and most elegant creations of Frederican Rococo.

With its rigorous mural arrangement – there are no panels or ornamental additions – the White Hall conveys an impression of severity and coolness. Only the light-filled ceiling painting, with its architectural concave edging by Friedrich Wilhelm Höder, affords some decorative relief in the rigorous overall structure. Originally, there had been plans to adorn the tops of the window arches with festoons or shell-ornaments. This is revealed in the ornamental additions which Nahl made to a sketch by Knobelsdorff. That this was not ultimately done may have been due to a desire to set up a conscious decorative contrast between the White Hall and the Golden Gallery, the great ballroom-cum-music-room, which adjoined it to the east. To enter this was to enter a different world: the dream-realm of an imaginary garden-party. The walls are lined with green imitation marble which acts as a foil for the subtle, mysterious interplay between a series of elaborate gilded grotesques. These were based on engravings by Antoine Watteau, Oppenordt, and La Joue, whose formal components Knobelsdorff translated into his own style.

The only person who could conceivably have been responsible for this multi-layered festive decoration, reminiscent of the convolutions of a Bach fugue, was the architect Georg Wenceslaus von Knobelsdorff. In collaboration with the best decorative artists at Friedrich's court – Johann August Nahl the Elder and Johann Michael Hoppenhaupt the Elder – he created one of the finest festive halls of European Rococo. There is no other example in the Frederican palaces of this kind of juxtaposition of two great halls linked to each other by their decorative style – a banqueting-hall with an architectural emphasis, and a ballroom-cum-music-room of ornamental character. It is therefore not surprising that Frederick the Great continued to use these rooms for court festivities long after he had transferred his residence to Potsdam.

What prompted Friedrich to favour Potsdam is not clear. The pastor at Charlottenburg – a man by the name of Dressel – cites various reasons in his parish chronicle. The king, for example, did not like the fact that several foreign emissaries had settled in Charlottenburg on account of the good air there; he did not want any informers in the environs. In addition, as Dressel also explains, Friedrich was a lover of the beauties of nature, 'and since Potsdam had several hills round it,

New Wing, door in White Hall leading to Golden Gallery

New Wing, White Hall, Friedrich II's former banqueting-hall and throne room. It was possible to copy the cornice painting from Friedrich Wilhelm Höder (d. *c.* 1761), but the ceiling painting, *The Wedding of Peleus and Thetis* by Antoine Pesne (1683–1757), originally dating from 1742, was destroyed in the war and was replaced in 1972–3 by a contemporary paraphrase by Hann Trier (b. 1915).

New Wing, view into the Golden Gallery
from the west

New Wing, Golden Gallery
Flora and her retinue over the entablature of the
western chimney-wall

New Wing, *sopraporta* over the north-west door of
the Golden Gallery
This detail gives a vivid impression of the lavish
ornamentation in this ballroom-cum-banqueting-hall.
The motif is inspired by the grotesque ornamental
designs of Antoine Watteau (1684–1721)

New Wing, Golden Gallery, console mirror on north wall

and, being an island, was surrounded by water, it was easier for the king to show nature off to good advantage there'. Furthermore, in Potsdam he was, said Dressel, 'further away from the din of the world' than in Charlottenburg or Berlin.

Memories of Friedrich's days as crown prince in Rheinsberg undoubtedly also had a decisive influence on his choice of Potsdam as his future residence. And yet the decision cannot have been an easy one for him to make: the resources expended on the Charlottenburg residence had been considerable. Knobelsdorff, for example, had been instructed to allow the greatest possible *magnificence* to prevail when it came to the decoration of the Golden Gallery. The glass used for the panes in this room, for instance, was not the usual window-glass, but better-quality, more expensive plate-glass.

In 1742, Friedrich had acquired, in Paris, the collection of antiquities belonging to Cardinal Polignac, and these were used mainly to decorate the New Wing. A total of twenty-two busts were assigned to the Golden Gallery. These were placed in twos on pedestals in front of each pilaster. All the pedestals were incrusted in a highly individual way with marble of various colours, probably taken from the marble slabs which formed part of the collection. As already mentioned, sixteen further busts decorated the south wall of the royal library, placed on large, lavishly decorated, silvered consoles; and one bust topped off the western and eastern *sopraporte* in this room. The artistically most important items in the Polignac collection – the eight life-sized figures that made up the piece known as the *Family of Lycomedes* – were positioned in the White Hall, on high white marble pedestals.

Frederick the Great's Second Apartment

In 1747, immediately after the completion of the Golden Gallery, the king had a second apartment arranged for himself at the eastern end of the New Wing. This consisted of a Concert-Room, a Gris-de-Lin Room, a Study, and a Bedchamber, but it served more as a picture-gallery. The first three rooms in particular were lavishly decorated with paintings. Most of these, however, fell victim to the depredations which the palace suffered at the hands of the Austrians and Cossacks in 1760.

The work was carried out under the supervision of the Hoppenhaupt brothers, probably working to existing plans drawn up by Johann August Nahl the Elder, who had fled Prussia in the summer of 1746. The standard here no longer matches that of Friedrich's First Apartment. The decorations already fall within

Jean-Baptiste Siméon Chardin (1699–1779)
The Cook
Oil on canvas, *c.* 1738

the second phase of Frederican interior design, which is marked by a certain decline in creativity.

The most impressive room in the apartment is probably the Concert-Room, sumptuously hung with paintings. It adjoins the Golden Gallery on the eastern side. The most remarkable item in it is Watteau's masterpiece, the *Enseigne de Gersaint* ('Shop-Sign of the Art-Dealer Gersaint'), painted in 1720 and acquired by Friedrich in 1745 specifically to hang in this spot, where it remains today. The picture was originally arc-shaped, but was extended into a rectangle and divided in the middle shortly after its creation.

In Frederick the Great's time, more than twenty paintings hung in this room. In 1760, however, when the palace was looted by the Cossacks and Austrians, the pictures suffered considerable damage. The jewels of the collection as it exists at present include: the *Dance in the Garden Room* and *Le Moulinet*, two major works by Nicolas Lancret; a landscape by Jean-Baptiste Pater, and *The Cook* (1738) by Jean-Baptiste-Siméon Chardin. Notable examples of Frederican furniture are the two cedar-wood commodes with bronze fittings and imitation-marble tops dating from 1745.

The original wall-covering of pale violet (*gris-de-lin*) damask in the next room was re-created after the war. So too was the gilded edging, with its elaborately carved corner cartouches. Some of Watteau's major works are currently on display here: *The Shepherds*, *Love in the Country*, and the famous *Embarkation for the Island of Cythera* (1719), which Friedrich only acquired between 1752 and 1765, when he had already turned his attentions away from Watteau and his school.

Friedrich's Study, which adjoins the Gris-de-Lin Chamber, is a panelled room. The gilded decoration on white ground was probably done to a design drawn up by the Hoppenhaupt brothers themselves. Originally, there were five paintings by Pesne, Lancret, and Dubois set into the walls. These were destroyed during the Seven Years War (1756–63) and were later replaced with four paintings by Christian Wilhelm Ernst Dietrich. The panels that now take their place were executed in 1746 for Prince August of Prussia, a brother of Frederick the Great. They are by Pesne, Knobelsdorff, Dubois, and Harper.

The last room in the apartment was the Royal Bedchamber, which was lined with green damask. The room is currently arranged more as a museum area, the chief exhibits being various *fêtes galantes* by Pater and Lancret, together with François Boucher's *Venus, Mercury, and Cupid*. A notable illustration of the high quality of Frederican cabinet-making is the simple, elegantly proportioned cedar-wood corner-cupboard with gilded bronze fittings. It was made in 1745 to a design by Knobelsdorff.

Antoine Watteau (1684–1721)
The Embarkation for the Island of Cythera
Oil on canvas, 1719
Frederick the Great acquired this famous painting
– the first version of which hangs in the Louvre –
between 1752 and 1765 for the western guest-suite in
the Stadtschloß in Potsdam.

New Wing, view into the 'Gris-de-Lin' Chamber in
Friedrich II's Second Apartment
The room derived its name from the pale violet
damask wall-covering (restored).

New Wing, king's study in the Second Apartment,
probably to a design by the Hoppenhaupt brothers

Pages 62–63:
Antoine Watteau (1684–1721)
L'Enseigne de Gersaint
Oil on canvas, 1720
Frederick the Great acquired this painting – Watteau's last work – in 1745 for the Concert Room in his Second Apartment in the New Wing. The picture, painted in a great hurry by Watteau for his friend the art-dealer Gersaint, was intended as a sign for the latter's shop, situated on the Pont Notre-Dame in Paris.

In the latter part of his reign, Friedrich lodged in Charlottenburg only for family celebrations, or for performances of operas and comedies, which he staged in the western Orangery. Otherwise, he stayed at Charlottenburg only when inspecting his troops at the drill-grounds in the Tiergarten, in Wedding, or in Spandau. The last time he was in the palace appears to have been in 1773. At that time, the town was already thoroughly depopulated. Charlottenburg's fame had faded. Many craftsmen had left the town, or had become day-labourers, because they could find no work. Pastor Dressel reported that when he visited Charlottenburg in 1770, he had met only a handful of people in the streets, and that these had not been outsiders but 'people in everyday clothes' – in other words, locals. 'In the palace garden I met just as few people as I had done years before: the gardener's lad at the garden gate was the first and last person we saw.'   TE

Cedar-wood corner-cupboard in the former Bed-chamber in Frederick the Great's Second Apartment. With its delicate proportions, this cupboard, designed by Georg Wenceslaus von Knobelsdorff (1699–1753) in about 1745, embodies the high-point of Frederican furniture-making.

François Boucher (1703–70)
Venus, Mars, and Cupid
Oil on canvas, *c.* 1742

Nicolas Lancret (1690–1745)
The Dance in the Garden Room
and *Le Moulinet*
Oil on canvas, *c.* 1720
Le Moulinet, which formerly hung in the Neues Palais
in Potsdam, is – like *The Dance in the Garden Room* –
one of the artist's major works. The *Moulinet* is a
figure in the *contredanse*, a kind of quadrille in which,
as the name implies, the couples dance in opposite
directions rather than, as in round dances, behind one
another. The *contredanse* had been a favourite
ballroom-dance since the beginning of the 18th
century.

65

Friedrich Wilhelm II
and Charlottenburg

 hen Friedrich Wilhelm II acceded to the throne on 17 August 1786, he was warmly welcomed by the populace because he abolished many unpopular measures to which they had latterly been subjected under the old king. He radiated kindness and good will and delighted those around him with his gifts and favours. His predecessor, however, did not have a very high regard for him. Following the death of his younger brother August Wilhelm, Friedrich had indeed designated the latter's son 'Prince of Prussia' and thus also his successor; however, he soon became aware of the prince's tendency to sexual excess, and his incapacity for hard work. The prince's vacillation in political matters soon became evident. A regime of favouritism and petticoat government established itself, with negative repercussions in every sphere.

However, the relaxation which occurred in the system of government that had prevailed under Frederick the Great also brought with it a new blossoming in social and cultural life. Numerous improvements in the domains of the law, taxation, education, and the military were initiated by Friedrich Wilhelm.

The new king had a deep understanding of music – he had personal links with Haydn, Mozart, and Boccherini, and later also with Beethoven – and he was a great promoter of German-language theatre. His short, eleven-year reign also signalled a new beginning for the plastic arts.

Whereas Frederick the Great had, to the last, clung to long-outdated rococo forms, an elegant early classicism now began to establish itself. Amongst its major artistic achievements during the 1780s were the interior decorations created in the Marble Palace at Potsdam and in the Royal Palace (Königskammer) by Friedrich Wilhelm von Erdmannsdorff (1736–1800), Karl von Gontard (1751–1791), and Karl Gotthard Langhans (1732–1808). Their elegant proportions and fine detail mark a high point in German early classicist interior decoration.

Anton Graff (1736–1813)
Portrait of Friedrich Wilhelm II (1744–97)
Oil on canvas, c. 1792

The Grounds

During the latter period of Frederick the Great's reign, the palace and grounds had been more or less left to their own devices. All this changed under the next monarch, Friedrich Wilhelm II. Charlottenburg was well known to the unloved nephew long before his accession to the throne in 1786. Here, close by the palace, on the banks of the Spree, he had, many years ago, bought a property for his mistress Wilhelmine Encke, later Countess Lichtenau. Over the years this had been extended into a substantial site. Friedrich Wilhelm II was very open to the

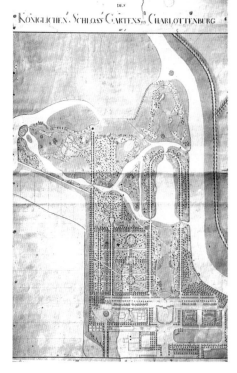

Georg Steiner (1774–1834)
Large-scale site-plan for the alterations to the grounds
of Charlottenburg Palace, 1812

mystificatory trends of his time, and in 1781, the palace was the location of his solemn admission to the Rosicrucian order.

After his accession to the throne, Friedrich Wilhelm continued to take a lively interest in the further development and extension of Charlottenburg, especially the transformation of the grounds into an English landscape garden. The degree of this interest is revealed in an observation made by Dressel in his parish chronicle, published in 1813: 'Friedrich Wilhelm II himself took up an axe and showed his gardener Johann August Eyserbeck, whom he had summoned from Wörlitz, how low he wanted the hedges pruned to improve the view.'

The grounds were now rearranged on the lines of the English-style gardens in Anhalt. The biggest task was the rearrangement of the great baroque *parterres*. The various sections in these were now combined into a broad lawn and planted with Weymouth pines and poplars. Because of their height, these trees – brought from Wörlitz – were a good foil to the old lindens that were already in place. In addition, they had great atmospheric value in terms of the new Romantic ideal.

Meanwhile, *bosquet* in the old garden retained its geometric shape, but an attempt was made to relieve its formality by adding winding paths. With the same object in mind, the straight edges of the carp-pond were 'undulated' and the outer dikes, already 'romantically' silted up, were helped along by being further narrowed artificially. A number of new bridges were also built after 1787. The two statues of the Great Elector and Elector Friedrich III installed in front of the garden façade by Frederick the Great were now removed.

An attractive addition to the garden was a pair of small fishing-huts erected not far from the palace, on the banks of the Spree. One was a tiny house, clad in wickerwork on the outside and decorated with 'Etruscan-style' painted canvas on the inside. This was located in the Hermitage Garden. The other was an airy pavilion in fantastical Gothic style, situated near the old bridge over the Spree and forming a Romantic *point de vue*. Both buildings were demolished at the end of the nineteenth century because of their dilapidated condition.

The Belvedere

The island formed to the north of the carp-pool by the River Spree and a branch leading off it was also transformed. Its main architectural feature now became the Belvedere, a three-storey structure on an oval base. The architect of this building, which was constructed in 1788 and combined baroque and classical elements, was Karl Gotthard Langhans, the designer of the Brandenburg Gate.

The Belvedere was destroyed in the war and has since been rebuilt. The interior decoration on the ground floor was extremely plain, that on the two upper floors more lavish. The walls of the oval hall on the first floor, for example, were panelled with yew and 'motley species of wood', and the ceiling was painted *en arabesque*. As in Friedrich Wilhelm II's winter apartments, furnished in 1796–7, the floor, by Johann Christoph Fiedler, was sumptuous. Various sorts of wood were used to create a three-dimensional rhomboid pattern; the central section contained arabesques, and the edging was decorated with rosettes. Curtains of blue *gros-de-Tour* with 'motley' fringes hung at the windows and doors.

The decoration in the oval hall on the second storey was equally lavish. The panelled walls were painted to resemble porphyry and were lacquered. White-lacquered consoles with gilded carvings bore eight large and sixteen small antique vases made of fired bronzed clay. At the windows hung curtains of red silk.

The Belvedere, formerly situated on an island in the palace grounds, was built in 1788 to a design by Karl Gotthard Langhans (1732–1808). View from the west Since 1972, the Belvedere has housed the Porcelain Museum, devoted to the history of Berlin porcelain.

The Theatre

Friedrich Wilhelm II was not only a great lover of music; he was also very fond of the theatre, especially German-language drama. Under Frederick the Great, the majority of plays performed were French. The moment Friedrich Wilhelm II assumed power, he took steps to ensure that works by classical German playwrights which had been spurned by 'der Alte Fritz' – Lessing's *Emilia Galotti* and Schiller's *Don Carlos*, for example – were now performed. Given his passion for drama, it is hardly surprising that the king should have had a theatre built at Charlottenburg.

The plans for this imposing building, completed between 1788 and 1791 and measuring 50 metres in length and 20 metres in depth, were drawn up by Karl Gotthard Langhans. He added the building on to the western end of Eosander Göthe's Orangery in such a way that it was accessible from inside. There was thus covered access from the palace to the theatre. The mansard roof and treatment of the façade reveal a continuing debt to baroque architecture; but there are some classicist elements too – notably the design of the central projection in the form of a portico topped with a Palladian motif.

The interior of the theatre, which is now used as a museum, had already been completely altered in 1902, when the building was converted into a furniture store. According to surviving sketches and photos, the auditorium had three circles of seating with a projecting royal box at the centre; the circles themselves were supported on palm-like consoles. The ceiling painting was by the Scottish

69

Karl Gotthard Langhans (1732–1808)
Theatre building at the west end of the Orangery,
seen from the south, 1788–91

painter Edward Francis Cunningham. In 1784, after an eventful life, Cunningham had settled in Berlin, where he came to prominence chiefly as a portraitist. The painting depicted a huge cloud-filled sky stretching out over a balustrade and peopled by hovering *putti* holding garlands of flowers. The remaining decoration was executed in very dark colours, and the gilding was tempered with yellow veneer and silver. The overall impression created by the interior of the theatre must have been a rather cool one.

Friedrich Wilhelm II's Summer Apartment

Two years after assuming power, Friedrich Wilhelm II had a Summer Apartment arranged for himself on the ground floor of the New Wing, in several rooms on the garden side which had previously formed part of Elisabeth Christine's suite. The apartment comprised five rooms in all, one of which was shaped like a long gallery. The suite begins with a room in which the ceiling was painted in the style of Etruscan vases by the Berlin artist Johann Gottfried Niedlich. The walls were originally lined with green-toned wallpaper edged with arabesques. It acted as a background for twenty-one English colour-engravings, five of which were after paintings by the Swiss history-painter Johann Heinrich Fuseli (1741–1825).

To the east of this lies the four-windowed Gallery mentioned above. It was

New Wing, Chinese Gallery in Friedrich Wilhelm II's
Summer Apartment, view from the west

painted in the Chinese style by Bartolomeo Verona. The ornamental mural and ceiling painting, much of which is original, and the carved mirror-frame and furniture are rather dry and bizarre in form, but are enlivened by their colourfulness. The walls were lined with paper painted with Chinese landscapes. Only fragments of this survive. The furnishings also included three colourful console-tables that match the decoration, two sofas, and twelve mahogany chairs. The Chinese decoration in the small adjoining room at the eastern end matched that of the Gallery. The original Chinese-style wallpaper disappeared during the Second World War and was replaced with paper of a similar design.

The neighbouring bedroom was also furnished in Chinese style. Its ceiling had been painted with Chinese figures *en arabesque* by Johann Gottfried Niedlich, and the walls of the anteroom were lined with Chinese-style paper. This room and the next one – lined with blue paper and decorated in Etruscan style – were destroyed during the war.

Friedrich Wilhelm II's Winter Apartment (the 'Winter Chambers')

Compared with Friedrich Wilhelm II's other accommodation, his Summer Apartment in Charlottenburg's New Wing was kept deliberately simple in character. Lavish wall-decorations of the kind typical of this monarch's usual domestic style will be sought in vain here, as will classicizing features. The bizarre-cum-rustic character of the apartment indicates that the king intended to lodge here only on occasional summer visits. It was probably not long before he felt the need to create another apartment – on the upper storey of the New Wing – which would be suitable for winter visits. A total of seven rooms previously forming part of Frederick the Great's First Apartment and located on the south side of the New Wing were chosen for this purpose.

The works began in summer 1796 and were completed one year later, in the year of the king's death. The identity of the main designer is not known. The archival sources name only the craftsmen who carried out the work. Most of these are cabinet-makers, the majority unknown. The only well-known figures from the artistic scene in Berlin and Potsdam are the decorative artists Johann Gottfried Niedlich, Johann Christoph Kimpfel, and Friedrich Bock. However, it is likely that the king's mistress, Countess Lichtenau, exerted the same kind of influence on the decoration of this suite as she had on that of the little castle on the Pfaueninsel (Peacock Island).

In the Second World War, the Winter Chambers were completely destroyed except for two rooms in the western area of the New Wing. Since many of the original furnishings had survived the war unscathed, it was decided, at the beginning of the 1980s, that the remaining rooms should be rebuilt on the basis of available building-records and surviving drawings and photographs.

The Winter Chambers at Charlottenburg occupy a special place amongst the various apartments which Friedrich Wilhelm II created in the course of his eleven-year reign. Compared with the rooms in the Marble Palace at Potsdam (1787–90), with their antique-style grotesques and plethora of lavish paintings, and compared with the king's suite (Königskammer) created in 1787–8 in the Royal Palace, the decoration in the Winter Chambers is less imposing. Panelled rooms alternate with rooms lined with painted silk. The ceiling paintings by Antoine Pesne or his pupil Harper which had been part of the decoration in Fred-

New Wing, Chinese Chamber in Friedrich Wilhelm II's Summer Apartment, view from the east

erick the Great's time were simply taken over, with new painting in the style of the time being provided for the surrounding cornices. A notable decorative element were the filigree chandeliers with glass hangings, which gave each room its own special touch.

In contrast to the wall-decoration, the flooring – a combination of sophisticated and complex patterns – was lavish. A host of different types of native and exotic woods were used: oak and mahogany, plum, elm, and maple, American walnut, mulberry, and ebony. In addition, the colour of some of the woods was modified by means of stain. The only other place in Prussia in which interior decoration of this order was to be found was the castle on the Pfaueninsel, which the king had created more for private use in 1790.

Despite the private nature of the Charlottenburg apartment – or perhaps precisely because of it – the co-ordination of ceiling, wall, and floor design radiates a discreet elegance that somehow echoes Frederican interior decoration.

Furnishings also played a special role in the Winter Chambers. Of particular note, in addition to the famous Don Quijote tapestries – about which more will be said later – were the various items of showpiece furniture. One such was the rare mahogany secretaire that was part of the apartment's original furnishings. It was made by the Berlin cabinet-maker Stein, as his test-piece for the status of master ('masterpiece').

A special feature of the Winter Chambers is their marbled clay stoves. Their untramelled, quasi-architecturally rigorous definition of space betrays the influence of the Berlin architects Friedrich Gilly and Heinrich Gentz, who were deeply affected by the French Revolution. All the stoves are shaped into a kind of pedestal and are decorated with fittings of bronzed clay in the shape of antique figures; the sides are adorned with bronzed gem-like oval reliefs or Egyptian-style sphinxes. The mere positioning of the stoves in the centre of the small wall in each room heightens their impact. They were produced in the factory founded by Johann Gottfried Höhler in 1780. The factory was taken over in 1812 by Christoph Tobias Feilner, and out of it developed the famous Feilner earthenware manufactory, which produced the ornamental and sculptural fittings for many of the buildings designed by Schinkel and his followers.

Access to the royal quarters was from the main staircase in the New Wing. One first passed through two mahogany-panelled rooms – the Haute-Lisse or High Warp rooms, so called on account of the famous Don Quijote tapestries that hung here. Frederick the Great's brother, Prince Heinrich, had received the six-piece set of tapestries, based on cartoons by Antoine Coypel, as a gift on the occasion of his visit to the Manufacture Royale de Meubles de la Couronne in Paris in 1784. He had later passed them to Friedrich Wilhelm II to decorate the Winter Chambers.

The tapestries depict scenes from Cervantes' story of Don Quijote, picked out against a crimson background and framed with an elaborate grotesque design. Only four tapestries have survived. These are now divided between the two rooms. In the first Haute-Lisse Room the tapestry scenes were supplemented with an oval ceiling painting depicting Don Quijote tilting at the windmills. This was painted by Johann Christoph Kimpfel, who was responsible for various ceiling paintings in the Marble Palace at Potsdam and in the king's chambers at the Royal Palace. The highly decorative *sopraporte* in both rooms – vases of exotic flowers set in niches – were painted by Friedrich Bock, who is otherwise better known as a portraitist.

New Wing, fragment of late 18th-century Chinese wall-covering in the Chinese Gallery in Friedrich Wilhelm II's Summer Apartment

New Wing, Winter Apartment of Friedrich Wilhelm II,
First Haute-Lisse Room, with commode (1785) by
Johann Gottlob Fiedler (active in Berlin from 1769)
and one of the four Don Quijote tapestries. The latter
depicts the scene where Don Quijote is cured of his
foolishness.

New Wing, Winter Apartment of Friedrich Wilhelm II, view into the Second Haute-Lisse Room from the west. On the walls hang three of the surviving Don Quijote tapestries made by the Gobelin workshops at Paris and given by Louis XVI to Prince Heinrich of Prussia, Frederick the Great's brother, in 1784.

Adjoining these rooms to the west is the Bedchamber with maple-wood panelling and painted yellow silk wall-covering. In Frederick the Great's time it was lined with yellow *drap d'argent*. The old ceiling painting – *Venus and Cupid* – by Antoine Pesne was left in place at the time of the alterations, a new edging of classicizing coffer-painting being merely added round it. Like the rest of the ceiling paintings from the time of Frederick the Great, it was destroyed during the Second World War.

Passing through a portal-like structure decorated with gilded carvings and topped with a classicizing *grisaille* painting, the visitor entered the now-destroyed Alcove Room, the ceiling of which was painted by the Berlin history painter and designer Johann Gottfried Niedlich.

The painted silk wall-covering in the Bedchamber was restored in a process

requiring great effort and expense. Its lively colour forms the perfect background to a set of court portraits of very high quality executed by Johann Heinrich Schröder.

The original furnishings in this room – a sofa, four chairs, an armchair, and a tabouret – are of walnut made to resemble bamboo. Such exotic 'camouflage' is typical of the phase of West Indies nostalgia that occurred in Friedrich Wilhelm II's time, sparked off mainly by Bernardin de Saint-Pierre's *Paul et Virginie*. It is often found in more rustic interiors – like that in the castle on the Pfaueninsel, which looks out over a Havel landscape rendered exotically alien by the presence of palm-trees.

In the next room – the elm-panelled royal Study – the grey-blue silk wall-covering painted with exotic flowers has not yet been restored. At present, the room contains an important collection of paintings by Anton Graff (1736–1813), including the portrait of Friedrich Wilhelm II and his daughter Friederike of Prussia, painted in 1787–8, and the picture of Frederick the Great's consort, Elisabeth Christine, in her later years, painted in 1789.

The restoration of the flower-patterned chintz wall-covering in the adjoining New Calico Dressing-Room, the last room in the suite, is also still to be completed. The ceiling in this room, like the walls, was covered with fabric, giving the room the air of an exotic enclosed garden pavilion.

Friedrich Wilhelm II was never able to take up residence in his Winter Apartment at Charlottenburg, completed in 1797. Stricken with dropsy, he visited the palace for the last time in the summer of that year. A performance of the German comedy *Die Zauberin Sidonia* was given in the theatre, in the presence of the Turkish ambassador. The sight of the king, sorely afflicted with dropsy, aroused great pity, reports Pastor Dressel in his chronicle. On 16 November 1797, Friedrich Wilhelm II died, aged 53, in the Marble Palace in Potsdam.   TE

New Wing, Winter Apartment of Friedrich Wilhelm II, view of the king's bedroom, with pastel portraits by Johann Heinrich Schröder (1757–1812)

Friedrich Wilhelm III

 n 16 November 1797, Friedrich Wilhelm II's eldest son, aged 27, acceded to the throne as Friedrich Wilhelm III. His forty-three-year reign – one of the longest in Prussia's history – was marked by momentous political, social, and economic changes, which also had a profound effect in the domains of art and culture.

The French Revolution and Napoleon's aggressive policy of expansion spelled the end for the old-style Prussia, which, at the turn of the century, was still strongly under the influence of Frederick the Great. The catastrophic defeat at the dual battle of Jena and Auerstädt on 14 October 1806 placed Prussia in mortal danger. In the 1807 Peace of Tilsit, whose terms were dictated by Napoleon, Friedrich Wilhelm III was obliged to forgo all the Prussian territories west of the Elbe and the lands in the east which his father had acquired as a result of the Second and Third Partition of Poland in 1793 and 1795. Prussia lost about half its territory and population. Massive contributions amounting to 120 million francs, combined with Napoleon's Continental System – the anti-British embargo on all overseas trade – led Prussia into economic ruin as well. In this situation, the forces that were pressing for a reform of the outdated absolutist state got their chance. The principal minister Baron Stein, the chancellor Baron Hardenberg, and the deputy chief of the general staff Scharnhorst quickly introduced reforms from above. The Wars of Liberation of 1813–14 and the Congress of Vienna in 1815 led to Prussia's regaining military and political strength and joining the ranks of the leading European powers within the framework of the 'Holy Alliance' with Russia and Austria. Following this, reform was replaced by a mood of reaction and restoration. Liberal, national, and – even more so – democratic ideas were suppressed; their advocates were muzzled and persecuted. Most of the reform legislation, however, remained intact.

At the same time, the expansion of government administration continued apace, and important first steps were taken in regard to technical and industrial advance. The arts and sciences also received a great boost with the foundation of academies, universities (Berlin, Breslau, Bonn), museums, and theatres. Berlin in particular, which was gradually developing into a metropolis, became a cultural hub and magnet for artists, writers, and scholars. In the plastic arts, Karl Friedrich Schinkel (1781–1840) – one of the most outstanding and multi-talented figures of the whole of Prussian history – was the determining influence. With buildings such as the Neue Wache on Unter den Linden (1817–18), the theatre on the Gendarmenmarkt (1819–21), the Museum am Lustgarten (1824–30), the church on the Werdersche Markt (1825–30), and the Academy of Architecture

Franz Krüger (1797–1857)
Portrait of Friedrich Wilhelm III (1771–1840),
with Charlottenburg in the background
Oil on canvas, c. 1835

Friedrich Georg Weitsch (1758–1828)
Friedrich Wilhelm III and Queen Luise in the grounds
of Charlottenburg Palace
Oil on canvas, 1799

opposite the palace (1832–6, now destroyed), he changed the face of central Berlin. Schinkel worked not only as an architect, but also as a painter and designer of stage-sets, ceremonial and interior decoration, furniture and lighting, and even vases and picture-frames. He thus exerted a great influence on every aspect of the taste and style of his age.

Christian Daniel Rauch (1777–1857) was the leading sculptor of the time, alongside Johann Gottfried Schadow (1764–1850). With his statues of the generals of the Wars of Liberation (1819–22) at the Neue Wache and the equestrian monument to Frederick the Great on Unter den Linden (1822–51), he made a major mark on the urban landscape.

Painting also flourished. The chief influences on Berlin painting of the Biedermeier period – in addition to Schinkel, whose architectural landscapes contain cul-

Carle Vernet (1758–1836)
The Consecration of the Prussian Flag on the Champ de Mars in Paris in 1814
Oil on canvas, 1822

Karl Friedrich Schinkel (1781–1841)
Cathedral, c. 1811
Oil on canvas
New (Schinkel) Pavilion

tural-philosophical, religious, and patriotic elements – were the portraitist and genre-painter Franz Krüger (1797–1857) and the architectural painter Carl Blechen (1797–1840). An important role was also played by Caspar David Friedrich (1774–1840). The Dresden master did not work in Berlin, but he exhibited regularly at the Academy and acquired an influential customer in Friedrich Wilhelm III.

If one enquires as to the contribution made by Friedrich Wilhelm III to the great developments of his time, it can hardly be said that this uncharismatic, constantly vacillating king exerted any decisive or trend-setting influence. In political matters, he simply reacted to events, followed the counsel of his ministers, or yielded to force of circumstance. He showed only a mediocre understanding of the great intellectual trends of his time; in contrast to Frederick the Great, or to his son, the future Friedrich Wilhelm IV, he had no interest in artistic issues or

Franz Krüger (1797–1857)
Friedrich Wilhelm III Inspects the First Regiment of Guards on Unter den Linden
Oil on canvas, 1839

questions of detail. And yet, when it came to commissions, he had a good instinct for supporting the many great talents which Prussia produced during the first half of the nineteenth century. In fact, thanks to the many progressive public building-schemes which Schinkel and others carried out under his regency, he actually became the author of 'modern Berlin'.

In his personal life he was modest and frugal. He tended towards a bourgeois life-style and felt most at home in his own family-circle, in the company of his wife, the much-revered Queen Luise, princess of Mecklenburg-Strelitz, whom he loved dearly, and of his many children. After his accession, he declined to move into the grandiose Royal Palace and remained in his old residence, the Crown Prince's Palace on Unter den Linden. The royal family's favoured places of residence, however, were Paretz, the Pfaueninsel, and Charlottenburg.

Jacques Louis David (1748–1825)
Napoleon Bonaparte as Consul, Crossing the Saint Bernard Pass
Oil on canvas, 1800

The important place which Charlottenburg occupied in the life of the royal family is clear from the fact that two of the children were born there, and were christened in the palace chapel: Princess Charlotte – who, as consort of Nicholas I, later became Tsarina Alexandra Feodorovna – was born there on 13 July 1798, and Prince Carl, creator of the palace at Glienicke, on 29 June 1801. The sons William, Carl, and Albrecht, and the daughter Luise were confirmed in the palace chapel; Prince Carl later married Princess Marie von Sachsen-Weimar there; and Friedrich Wilhelm III himself celebrated his second marriage at Charlottenburg.

The timing and duration of royal visits followed a fixed pattern. At the beginning of May, the royal couple would come to Charlottenburg for two or three days for the special review of the troops in the Tiergarten. From the middle of May – generally the 18th – they took up residence at the palace for several months. Finally, the king returned to the palace for one or two days at the start of the second half of September in order to take part in the daily field-exercises that were part of the autumn manœuvres.

During their visits, the royal couple occupied the western part of the New Wing built for Frederick the Great. Friedrich Wilhelm's rooms were located on the ground floor; Queen Luise's suite was above this, in Frederick the Great's so-called First Apartment. Since both apartments had only recently been rearranged in the latest style for Friedrich Wilhelm II, no major updating was needed. The changes made under Friedrich Wilhelm III were confined to small-scale measures such as the hanging of new curtains, the application of a new coat of paint, or the renewal of wallpaper. In the case of furnishings, recourse was often had to existing stocks, and use was made of items that had belonged to Friedrich Wilhelm II or Frederick the Great. This was the case with the six large bookcases from the Library in the First Apartment, which were now removed to the ground floor to accommodate Friedrich Wilhelm III's collection of books.

Friedrich Wilhelm III's apartment
Formerly the library of Friedrich Wilhelm III, now furnished with items (c. 1800) from the king's various apartments in Berlin and Potsdam.

Not until 1810, following the return of the royal couple from East Prussian exile in Königsberg on 23 December 1809, was there any major alteration of individual rooms. The young Schinkel, here employed for the first time by the royal house, was commissioned to redesign the queen's bedroom. Schinkel's plan envisaged a strictly symmetrical arrangement of furnishings, with a magnificent bed facing the window, and a bedside table on either side. The bed was to have elaborate carved decoration and pillars topped with guardian spirits. The spirits were intended to act as supports for a canopy formed from excess fabric wall-covering that was to be drawn out over the bed. The framework was to take the form of four tall pillars and a cornice. At regular intervals along this there were to be owls, and these were to have ribbons in their beaks to which the fabric was to be attached. The lavish, ostentatious-looking design was not executed. This may have been because the necessary resources were lacking, or because such a display of magnificence was felt to be inappropriate in the hard times then prevailing, or simply because the modest-sized room was considered unsuitable. The design that was actually executed was a much simpler one. The idea of a room entirely lined with fabric was retained, but the choice now was for a delicate white voile backed with pink paper; the gathering on this was to be flatter, and the covering was only to be applied to the walls, not drawn out into the room. The furnishings were also much simpler. These were to be made of pearwood and consisted of a bed mounted on a sort of 'step', two small tables, a sofa, and six upholstered chairs with back-rests and seats covered in embroidered muslin. Only the bed and two small tables have survived; the sofa and chairs have disappeared. For the bed, Schinkel used a French Empire design – the *lit-bateau* or 'ship-bed'; in this case, however, he did not include the characteristic outward-curving ends which Luise had already chosen in 1803 for her bedroom in the Crown Prince's Palace. The simple, very elegant carved decoration – an antique garland-motif with undulating ribbons – which perfectly accentuates the concave movement of the side panel, is also of French inspiration and was used at about the same time on a bed of state for the Empress Joséphine at Compiègne. The king's bedroom underwent similar alteration at the same time as the queen's.

Josef Grassi (1758–1838)
Queen Luise
Oil on canvas, 1802
New (Schinkel) Pavilion
Lent by the House of Hohenzollern

It was given a fabric wall-covering of pleated muslin over yellow-painted paper. Following changes made in the late nineteenth century, and the severe damage that occurred in the Second World War, only Queen Luise's bedroom has been restored to its original state, the lost seating having been replaced with other furniture from among Luise's possessions.

In Friedrich Wilhelm's apartments no entirely original items have been preserved, but numerous paintings, pieces of furniture, and other fittings convey a good impression of its former character. The paintings in particular include many notable items: portraits of the king and queen and their relatives, and of other important figures of the time, as well as battle scenes, genre pictures, and history paintings depicting events from the Wars of Liberation.

Amongst the portraits is a double likeness of the king and queen in the grounds of Charlottenburg Palace. This was painted in 1799 by Friedrich Georg Weitsch. At the Academy exhibition of 1800 it served as the keynote to a special section of patriotic history paintings and national landscapes specifically commissioned by the king. Notable amongst the portraits of Friedrich Wilhelm II is the great full-length likeness by Franz Krüger, which shows the already elderly king attending field-exercises near Charlottenburg. In the same room, directly opposite the king, there is a portrait of his great rival, Napoleon. It depicts the Emperor as First Consul and young general crossing the Great Saint Bernard pass on horseback. The portrait, of which several versions were made by Jacques-Louis David in 1800–1, was a gift from General von Blücher, who brought it back from Paris as booty in 1815. Ludwig Elsholtz's *Scene from the Battle before Paris on 30 March 1814* and Carle Vernet's *Consecration of the Prussian Flag on the Champ de Mars in Paris, 1814* tackle themes from the time of the Wars of Liberation against Napoleon. Both paintings formerly hung in the dining-room at the Crown Prince's Palace. This room, which contained other history paintings and portraits of generals, served as a kind of hall of remembrance commemorating the struggle against Napoleon. Vernet's *Consecration* also provided the inspiration for the famous series of parade paintings by Krüger, of which the *Parade on Unter den Linden* is a good example.

Karl Friedrich Schinkel (1781–1841)
Queen Luise's Bedroom in the New Wing, 1810

Karl Friedrich Schinkel (1781–1841)
First design for Queen Luise's bedchamber
(not executed)
Watercolour, 1809

The Mausoleum

The sudden death of Queen Luise on 19 July 1810 in Hohenzieritz was an event that deeply affected the whole of Prussia. The queen was not only widely admired and loved for her beauty and charm; because of her conduct after the defeat by the French, she was held up as an example in which the humiliated patriots saw the embodiment of Prussian moral superiority *vis-à-vis* the occupier. Leading Prussian artists therefore also gave committed support to the idea of creating a lasting memorial to her. However, it was the king himself who not only chose the location for the planned mausoleum but also decided substantially what form it should take. A rough ground-plan prepared by him showed a structure resembling a Doric temple, with a four-columned portico set over seven steps; behind this there was to be an inner vestibule with three flights of stairs, the middle one of which would lead to the vault containing the sarcophagus, and the two side ones to an upper memorial hall. Schinkel, who himself designed a Gothic-style columned hall through which the light could stream, was commissioned to translate the king's scheme into concrete form, producing drawings of the façade and rationalizing the design. Responsibility for the execution of the plans was handed over to the Royal Surveyor-General's Office, under the direction of the tried and tested royal surveyor Heinrich Gentz. Gentz managed to press ahead with the works at such a pace that the transfer of the body took place as early as 23 December 1810. The porch and all the structural components were made of sandstone treated with a light, warm-toned yellow wash; the walls were covered with ashlar facing and painted deeper yellow. For the columns of the portico, Schinkel chose a Hellenistic variation of the classic Doric order, distinguished by its especially slender proportions and only just coming into vogue. For the interior, the king made available four sumptuous jasper columns from Oranienburg. These were fitted with new bases and capitals of white Carrara marble and were made into a pair, set on high plinths. They were installed at the entrance to the memorial hall. For the stairways, column pedestals, and wall-plinths in the vestibule, red marble was used. Since the interior could not be entirely clad in marble, on account of the economic difficulties in which the country found itself, the walls were lined with greenish-grey and the cornice with yellowish imitation marble.

For the monument, which was to be positioned in the memorial hall, the king decided that the dead queen should be depicted lightly shrouded and recumbent on a sarcophagus-like base. He gave precise instructions as to posture: the upper body was to be raised, the head was to incline slightly to the right, the arms and legs were to be crossed. Designs were requested not only from the Berlin artists

Mausoleum of Queen Luise, porch
Design: Karl Friedrich Schinkel (1781–1841), 1810
Alterations in granite, 1828

Caspar David Friedrich (1774–1840)
Harbour View (Greifswald)
Oil on canvas, 1815
This painting, together with another that has since disappeared, was exhibited at the Dresden Academy Exhibition in 1816 and was also shown in Berlin in the same year. Both paintings were then purchased by Friedrich Wilhelm III and presented as a birthday gift to Crown Prince Friedrich Wilhelm (IV).

Christian Daniel Rauch (1777–1857)
Tomb of Queen Luise
Crestola marble (Carrara), 1811–14

Johann Erdmann Hummel (1769–1852)
Interior view of the Mausoleum with sarcophagus
design by Albrecht Dietrich Schadow (1797–1869)
Watercolour, 1810–11

Schadow and Rauch, but also from Canova and Thorwaldsen, the two most famous sculptors of their time. The king eventually opted for the design submitted by the as yet little-known Rauch, which combined the natural with the dignifiedly ideal. Rauch made the model for the monument in the presence of the king in the Orangery at Charlottenburg; the actual execution – in very fine yellow-gleaming Carrara marble – took place in Rome. Before his departure, Rauch had suggested to the king that two large marble candelabras be set either side of the monument. The monument and the candelabras arrived at Charlottenburg in May 1815, after an eight-month peregrination across the oceans, and were immediately installed in the Mausoleum. In 1828 the first alterations were made to the building: the sandstone façade was replaced with one of polished granite hewn from a block from the Mark of Brandenburg discovered shortly before. The sandstone portico was moved to the Pfaueninsel and a small open hall was added to it as a further memorial to the queen.

The New Pavilion (Schinkel Pavilion)

Fourteen years after the death of Luise, Friedrich Wilhelm III married again. On 9 November 1824 in the palace chapel at Charlottenburg he entered a morganatic union with the 27-year-old Auguste Countess of Harrach. He commissioned Schinkel to build a small summer residence for himself and his young wife (she acquired the title Princess of Liegnitz and Countess of Hohenzollern). This was situated in the eastern part of the palace grounds, behind the New Wing and not far from the River Spree. In accordance with the express wishes of the king, the building was modelled on the Villa Reale Chiatamone, where Friedrich Wilhelm had stayed during his visit to Naples in 1822.

The New Pavilion, which is built on a more or less square base, combines simplicity and clarity of structure with lightness and elegance of proportion. There are two storeys and a low tent-roof concealed behind the top ledge or attic. The upper storey has a balcony running round it. This is supported on cast-iron consoles and is provided with a simple railing. In the middle of each of the four façades there is a French window on the ground floor and a loggia on the upper floor. The west front, facing the palace terrace, and the east front, facing the Spree, have the added emphasis of wider loggias supported by two columns. The architectural components of the building – the bases, the capitals, the window tops, and the cornice – are made of sandstone, whilst the walls are rendered in red-tinged white, to which the bright green of the shutters provides a lively contrast.

Inside, each of the two floors is divided into nine almost identically sized units, though the loggias on the upper floor take up only half a unit, and the remaining spaces, in the guise of corridors and box-rooms, link the corner rooms with one another. The staircase is situated at the centre of the building and is accessible via the vestibule located on the south side.

Schinkel designed not only the building but also the interior decoration and many of the furnishings. The decoration was kept deliberately simple: most of the rooms had only single-colour wallpaper in red, yellow, green, blue, or white, with a patterned surround, and the curtains were white. The only exception was the west-facing garden-room on the ground floor near the staircase, which Julius Schoppe decorated with Pompeian grotesque paintings. Consisting of the equivalent of two units, this room was twice the size of the others. It had a very imposing kind of wall-decoration consisting of areas of multi-coloured imitation marble sectioned off by means of protruding edging and cornices. There were two fireplaces of white Carrara marble and – a particularly attractive feature – a wide semicircular niche into which a large bench was fitted, in the manner of an antique exedra. The side-rests of the white-painted wooden frame, with its griffin's feet, were modelled on a round bench at Pompeii. The bench was upholstered in blue silk rep (*gros d'Ispahan*), and the niche was lined with blue rep embroidered with yellow stars. Schinkel also furnished the other rooms with carefully selected furnishings and artefacts. Many of these he had made to his own design; but he also used existing items, including masterpieces of Russian craftwork which Tsarina Alexandra Feodorovna had sent as gifts to her father, and also artefacts which the king had brought back from Italy. Pictorial decoration was provided chiefly by engravings and drawings that were of personal sentimental value. These included forty-four engravings of works by Raphael, which were hung in what were known as the 'Green' and 'White' Rooms.

Christian Daniel Rauch (1777–1857)
Relief of second, morganatic consort of Friedrich Wilhelm III, Auguste Princess of Liegnitz
Carrara marble, 1838
New (Schinkel) Pavilion

New (Schinkel) Pavilion, executed 1824–5 by Albrecht Dietrich Schadow (1797–1869) to plans by Karl Friedrich Schinkel (1781–1841)

Albrecht Dietrich Schadow (1797–1869)
Sections through the New Pavilion
Pen, ink, watercolour, 1824–5
New (Schinkel) Pavilion

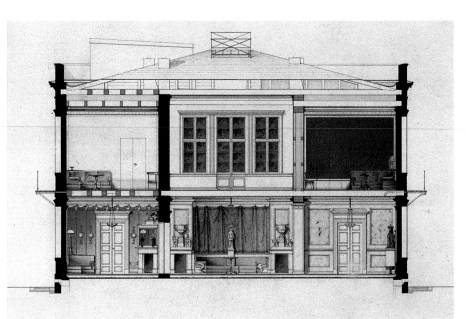

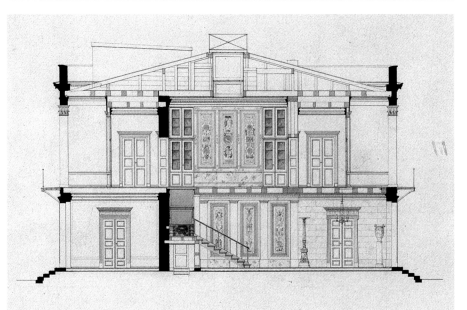

Gustav Bläser (1803–74)
*Tsarina Alexandra Feodorovna of Russia, formerly
Princess of Prussia, on Horseback*
Bronze with silver inlay, 1836
New (Schinkel) Pavilion

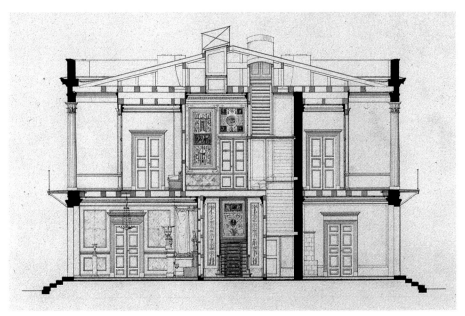

The Pavilion was burnt down on 23 November 1943; nothing but the external walls remained. Only a few fragments of the interior decoration survived. In the process of reconstruction that took place between 1957 and 1970, the structure and most of the internal fixtures were restored, but not the movable items. These were replaced, where possible, with comparable pieces from Schinkel's time. As a result, the Pavilion now houses a diverse collection of items that not only document the personal life-style of Friedrich Wilhelm III but also provide a good illustration of the artistic production of his time and of the leading artist in Prussia, namely Karl Friedrich Schinkel, whose name the Pavilion now bears.

The Pavilion's current furnishings comprise a rich collection of craft objects, including: a collection of Berlin iron and products of the Königliche Porzellanmanufaktur – KPM (Royal Porcelain Manufactory), which in those days was held in high artistic regard; a large number of small-scale figures, busts, and sculptures by Schadow, Rauch, and others; various watercolours and engravings (including some of Schinkel's famous designs for stage-sets); and, last but not least, a set of very fine paintings. In addition to two panoramas by Eduard Gaertner – the six-part *Berlin Panorama* of 1834, which offers a complete panorama of the city and surrounding area from the roof of the Friedrichswerdersche Kirche, and the three-part *Kremlin Panorama* painted in 1839 during a longish visit to Russia – the most notable items here are a number of works by Schinkel and Carl Blechen.

Karl Friedrich Schinkel (1781–1841)
Candelabra from the Oval Marble Hall in Prince Albrecht's Palace on the Wilhelmstrasse (destroyed)
Bronze, fire-gilt, 1831–2
New (Schinkel) Pavilion

Karl Friedrich Schinkel (1781–1841)
Garden Room in the New (Schinkel) Pavilion
1824–5

The Palace Grounds

Given the role of Charlottenburg as a summer residence, Friedrich Wilhelm III's interest in it encompassed not only the buildings but also the grounds. In 1819, Peter Joseph Lenné (1798–1866), the most renowned landscape architect of the nineteenth century, who also created the parks at Sanssouci, Potsdam, and Glienicke, was commissioned to transform the garden, which had retained its French-style baroque character, into a modern landscape garden. With the exception of the rectilinear avenues and large pool, which the king wished to preserve, Lenné completely broke up the garden's baroque layout. With the aid of Charlottenburg's royal gardener, Georg Steiner, he transformed part of the former *bosquets* into broad lawns, which he edged with an undulating line of bushes and projecting single trees. The regular system of paths was replaced with slightly curving footpaths, most of which ran round the edges of the grounds, but some of which cut across to the main avenues, creating multiple diagonal sight-lines and thus removing the cramped feel of the relatively narrow site. In 1828 Lenné began alterations to the *parterre* between the palace and the carp-pool. Avenues were added at the sides, with connecting paths leading to parallel longitudinal footways; four cross-paths were created which linked the two sides of the *parterre*. The plants that were introduced were made to follow the line of the paths, and the intersections were accentuated with dark clumps of trees. The main woody plants used were maple, poplar, cherry, willow, ash, birch, plane, and acacia in the way of trees, and, in the way of ornamental shrubs, broom, dwarf almond, hawthorn, quince, and honeysuckle. In 1837, in the area between the Luisenplatz and the palace, and not very far from the Pavilion, a flower garden was created for Princess Auguste.

Finally, under Friedrich Wilhelm III major changes were also made to the garden sculpture, and Christian Daniel Rauch was appointed to carry out a survey of existing sculpture here and in the gardens at Sanssouci and Potsdam. Rauch considered that the antique busts of Roman emperors which Frederick the Great had acquired as part of the Polignac collection and which were placed alongside the palace at Sanssouci were too valuable to be left on open display. They were therefore removed to the Museum in 1830, and eight of the baroque busts of emperors by Batholomäus Eggers which were lodged at Charlottenburg were brought to Sanssouci; twelve more went to the Neues Palais in Potsdam. Between 1822 and 1840, however, the park at Charlottenburg received nine important bronze statues; three of these were newly created by Rauch, and six were copies of famous antique sculptures.   RC

Charlottenburg Palace, garden front with palace pond, seen from the north

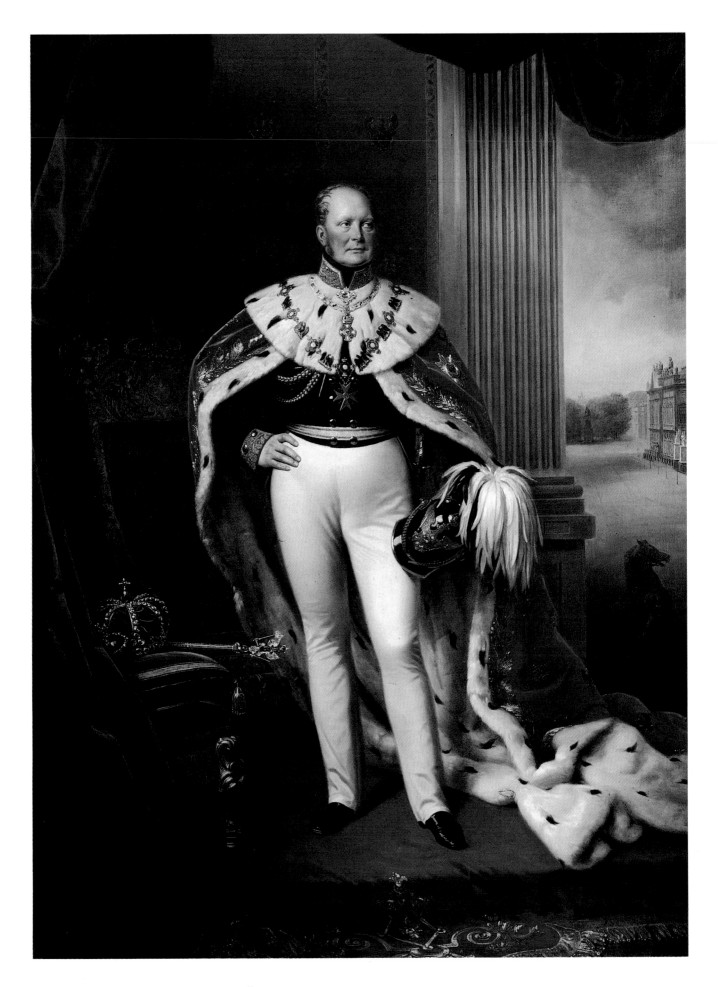

Friedrich Wilhelm IV
and Charlottenburg

 riedrich Wilhelm IV (1795–1861), who assumed the Prussian throne in 1840, was the last Hohenzollern monarch to have an apartment created for him at Charlottenburg, and the last to reside regularly at the palace. Every year, in late autumn and in the winter months from January, the king and his royal household would spend time at the palace. Particularly after the 1848 revolution, Friedrich Wilhelm tended to avoid what he himself called 'faithless Berlin', residing in nearby Charlottenburg and carrying out his royal duties from there. 'The life-style of the royal household at Charlottenburg was that of a *grand seigneur* in the country,' wrote Otto von Bismarck in his memoirs (*Gedanken und Erinnerungen*). Bismarck paid a visit to the king in Charlottenburg in April 1852 and reports further that he was offered a 'tasty and elegantly served breakfast' as compensation for a delay in his audience with the king.

Both palace and grounds at Charlottenburg were well known to the king. He had spent part of his childhood and youth here with his parents and siblings. Charlottenburg had provided a refuge to the royal family during the troubled times of the Napoleonic wars. Finally, following her untimely death, the king's mother, Queen Luise, had been laid to rest in the Mausoleum here, in the grounds of her favourite residence.

Friedrich Wilhelm IV, who in his time was already dubbed the 'Romantic on the throne', was an extremely cultivated monarch who showed great interest in the arts, and at the beginning of his reign he was the focus of many great hopes. However, his entire reign was dominated by the major political problems of the nineteenth century: growing industrialization, the social problem, the revolution of 1848, the national question, and, finally, the issue of Prussia's transition to constitutionality. From early on in his youth, the king showed a marked interest in his eminent forebear Frederick the Great. In addition, in contrast to the adherents of classicism, who rejected the whimsical rococo style, he developed a positive attitude to Frederican Rococo. This penchant for late baroque also reflects his espousal of the idea that the monarch has unlimited power and authority – although in the reality of everyday politics he was confronted, throughout his reign, with demands for a constitutional monarchy.

As crown prince, Friedrich Wilhelm IV had, through the efforts of his tutor Friedrich Delbrück, already become familiar with Frederick the Great's centres of activity at Potsdam, Berlin, and Charlottenburg. On visits to the various palaces he had lodged in the Frederican apartments. In 1815 the crown prince obtained permission from his father, Friedrich Wilhelm III, to use Frederick II's suite in the Royal Palace.

Eduard Gaertner (1801–77)
Charlottenburg Palace
Oil on canvas, 1846
View of garden façade of palace and western façade
of New (Schinkel) Pavilion
Lent by the House of Hohenzollern

Berlin School, after 1851
Official Portrait of King Friedrich Wilhelm IV
(1795–1861)
Oil on canvas

Joseph Stieler (1781–1858)
Queen Elizabeth of Prussia
Oil on canvas, 1843
Lent by the House of Hohenzollern

The Apartments of Friedrich Wilhelm IV and Queen Elisabeth

Only a short time after Friedrich Wilhelm IV had acceded to the throne on 7 June 1840, he decided to have accommodation arranged for himself and his consort, Queen Elisabeth (1801–1873), at Charlottenburg. The New Wing of the palace, which Frederick the Great had had built immediately after his accession and in which Friedrich Wilhelm III and Queen Luise had had an apartment, remained untouched. After the death of his father, Friedrich Wilhelm IV himself had had various mementos of his parents brought to Charlottenburg from the Crown Prince's Palace on Unter den Linden.

For both apartments the king chose rooms on the upper storey of the old palace. These had already been occupied by Friedrich Wilhelm I, the Soldier King, when he was crown prince, and by Frederick the Great until the New Wing was complete. The position on the upper storey also offered a panoramic and hugely attractive view over the palace grounds.

When the palace at Charlottenburg was destroyed during the Second World War, the apartments of Friedrich Wilhelm IV and Queen Elisabeth, done out in historicizing style, were consumed in the flames, together with some of the furnishings, paintings, and sculptures. The Library was the only room that it was possible to restore as an example of Friedrich Wilhelm IV's life-style at Charlottenburg. It was fitted out with pieces from the original stock of furniture, which had been evacuated to Potsdam and had survived. The remaining rooms of this apartment in the old palace have been arranged as museum areas for displaying outstanding works of art from the time of the Great Elector, Friedrich Wilhelm. The main items now on view in these rooms are the six tapestries from the eight-part set depicting the *Military Exploits of the Great Elector*. These were made in Philippe Mercier's workshop in Berlin in 1690–1700, at the request of Friedrich I, and they formerly hung in the Royal Palace. The cartoons for them were made by Rütger von Langerfeld, Joseph Franz, Alexander Casteels, Paul Leygebe, and Abraham Begeyn.

At the intersection of the two apartments lay the two great halls under the cupola: the Circular Hall facing the main courtyard, and the Oval Hall overlooking the palace grounds. The five rooms to the west of the halls were occupied by Friedrich Wilhelm. These were: the Adjutant's Room and Lecture Room on the garden side; and the Study, Library and Bedroom on the courtyard side. Queen Elisabeth's suite lay to the east of the central halls: the Tea Room and Ivory Room overlooking the garden, and the Library, Breakfast Room-cum-Study, and Bedroom-cum-Dressing-Room facing the main courtyard.

Carl Graeb (1816–84)
Lecture Room of Friedrich Wilhelm IV
Watercolour, c. 1855

Friederike Meinert (1836–48 at Berlin Academy
exhibitions)
Upper Oval Hall, view northwards towards the palace
grounds
Watercolour, 1843

Thanks to various inventories and to watercolours by Friederike Meinert, Friedrich Wilhelm Klose, and Carl Graeb, we have a good idea of how the apartments were arranged and furnished. Depiction of royal accommodation was common in nineteenth-century painting. The *Zimmermaler* ('room-painters'), as they were called, gave detailed and atmospheric renderings of the royal interiors. Such paintings were mostly given as gifts to members of the family and other relations. Today they provide important information about, and illustrations of, interior decoration and life-style in the first half of the nineteenth century.

The two great central halls were used for social functions. The Circular Hall was a dining-room and, according to the watercolour by Friederike Meinert, had windows decorated in Moorish style. Two cupboards fitted into the east and west walls contained an extensive and remarkable collection of glass from glassworks in Brandenburg. The collection was moved to the newly founded Hohenzollern Museum in Monbijou in 1877 but all trace of it has disappeared since the Second World War.

The Oval Hall served as a reception room. In front of the pilasters between the windows stood four monumental Russian porcelain vases made at the Imperial Porcelain Manufactory in St Petersburg. They were decorated with military scenes and were a gift from Tsar Nicholas I to the Prussian royal house. Also installed in this room were two console-tables dating from the beginning of the palace's construction, in about 1700. The bases of these were formed from gilded figures of slaves, topped off with a slab of white marble. On them stood two kraters made by the Sèvres manufactory – gifts from King Charles X of France.

Friedrich Wilhelm Klose (1804–after 1863)
Queen Elisabeth's library
Watercolour, c. 1845

The Adjutant's Room and Lecture Room in the king's apartment retained the rich gilded stucco ceiling and ceiling paintings from the original baroque room design. The walls were covered in unframed coloured paper and decorated with various fittings, mostly in the style of the second phase of Rococo.

The only room in Friedrich Wilhelm IV's apartment which it has been possible to restore since the destruction caused during the Second World War is the Library. The king regarded a library as part of the obligatory architectural canon in all royal palaces. He had been a collector of books from his early youth and had systematically built up an extensive collection. This ultimately became 'by far the richest and most diverse of the [Hohenzollern] libraries, from the point of view both of size and of content'. At his death in 1861, Friedrich Wilhelm IV left behind some 20,000 volumes. These were later to form the core of the Königliche Haus-

Library of King Friedrich Wilhelm IV (1795–1861)
Design by Johann Heinrich Strack (1805–80)
Executed 1845–6
Refurbished 1993

bibliothek (Royal Library), which until the Second World War was lodged in the Royal Palace and which brought together the private book collections of individual members of the Hohenzollern dynasty.

When the room was altered in 1845–6, parts of the original baroque decoration were preserved. These included the Old Testament scene in stucco relief depicting *Moses Raising the Brazen Serpent*, and sections of the stucco frieze and corona. The walls and window recesses were panelled in maple-wood. The bookcases were placed in front of the panelling. The upper parts of these are sectioned off by grooved pilasters. The flat panels of the doors on the lower parts are decorated with narrow straight or slightly curved convex beading.

The restored Library in Charlottenburg is not only 'a remarkable example of interior decoration from the post-Schinkel period, but also the last of the series of major Hohenzollern libraries from nineteenth-century Berlin' (Winfried Baer).

The two rooms on the garden side of Queen Elisabeth's apartment – the Tea Room (or 'Green-Panelled Room') and the Ivory Room ('Panelled Room') – previously formed part of Frederick the Great's temporary apartment. They still had wall-decoration executed by Friedrich Christian Glume in 1740. Glume played an important part in the decoration of Rheinsberg, where Friedrich resided as crown prince. In the 1862 inventory, which was drawn up after Friedrich Wilhelm IV's death, the Tea Room is described as follows: 'Green or Silver Room / 1. The walls are panelled, painted green, with oil-paint, and decorated with silvered carvings in the baroque French style; the floor is oak. Over the 3 doors there are 2 compositions of flowers and one of fruit painted in oil and enclosed in a silvered ornamental surround; the ceiling is painted white.'

The earlier Frederican wall-decoration had thus been left in place. The surviving watercolours of the room give a good impression of this unpretentious wall-carving, the chief feature of which is its clearly defined silvered or gilt sectioning, dissolving into an ornamental area in the upper half.

The decoration of the rooms with furniture, paintings, and craft objects was fully in line with the trend observable in all royal residences in the mid-nineteenth century. The furnishings comprised both original rococo pieces dating from the eighteenth century – including lacquered and Boulle-style items – and imitations of the second phase of Rococo. The royal apartment did, however, also contain decorative items from the early Charlottenburg period, round about 1700.

The complement of paintings chosen for the apartments was fully in keeping with the taste of its royal occupants. According to the inventory, most were either portraits of the royal family and their relations, or landscapes, or architectural works by contemporary artists. *Sopraporte* such as the flower-piece by Augustin Dubuisson (*c.* 1740) in Queen Elisabeth's room, were left in place.

When Friedrich Wilhelm IV died after a long illness in 1861 – his brother Prince William (1797–1888) had assumed the regency in 1858 – Queen Elisabeth chose Charlottenburg, along with Sanssouci, as the place in which to spend her widowhood, remaining there until her death on 14 November 1873.   TK

Paul Graeb (1842–92)
Ivory Room and Green Room in Queen Elisabeth's apartment, c. 1875 and 1869
Watercolour

The Emperor Friedrich

or a few months, from March to June 1888, Charlottenburg became an imperial residence. On their return from San Remo, the terminally ill Emperor Friedrich (1831–1888) and the Empress Victoria (1840–1901) resided at Charlottenburg before moving into the Neues Palais in Potsdam, where Friedrich died on 15 June 1888. He was the last Hohenzollern to use Charlottenburg as a place of residence.

The palace rooms were restored and made ready for the imperial couple, so that eminent official guests such as the English Queen Victoria, mother of Empress Victoria, could be accommodated. On 24 May 1888 the wedding of the emperor and empress's son Prince Heinrich to Princess Irene of Hesse took place in the palace chapel.

Historic photographs of the great state rooms provide a record of the baroque furnishings. In the Great Oak Gallery, the shelves (of carved gilded linden-wood, Berlin *c.* 1695) were filled with oriental porcelain from the Porcelain Room at Oranienburg; and pedestal-tables bearing oriental porcelain vases were placed in the window recesses. Antique oriental carpets were laid down the middle of the Gallery. Two large Frederican console-tables were placed in the Panelled Corner-Room beyond the Great Oak Gallery, and on small pedestals on top of

Heinrich von Angeli (1840–1925)
Kaiser Friedrich III as Crown Prince (1831–88)
Pastel, c. 1885

Great Oak Gallery. Photographed in 1888
During the short regency of Kaiser Friedrich III
the high-baroque shelvings for porcelain from
Oranienburg were transferred to the Gallery.

Panelled Corner-Room. Photographed in 1888 Frederican console-tables with items from the silver collection in the Rittersaal at the Royal Palace.

these were displayed items from the silver collection in the Rittersaal at the Royal Palace.

After the death of Emperor Friedrich, Charlottenburg Palace was used only for odd days as a royal residence, serving mainly as a venue to receive royal guests.

The Extension of the Mausoleum

When Friedrich Wilhelm III died on 7 June 1840, his son and successor, Friedrich Wilhelm IV, had his body placed next to that of his consort Queen Luise. In order for a monument in the form of the sleeping figure of the king to be erected, as in the case of Luise, the area had to be enlarged. The addition of an extra room to accommodate both monuments was carried out between 1841 and 1842 by Ferdinand Hesse, working to plans drawn up by Schinkel. Christian Daniel Rauch was

Erdmann Encke (1843–96)
Sarcophagus of Kaiser Wilhelm I, Mausoleum
Marble, 1890–4

commissioned to design a sarcophagus to match that of Queen Luise. At the end of 1842 Rauch had a design ready to present to Friedrich Wilhelm IV. In accordance with the king's wishes, Friedrich Wilhelm III was depicted in uniform. In August 1846 the sculpture was executed in white Carrara marble. The two monuments were placed in the enlarged Mausoleum later that year.

Friedrich Wilhelm IV had planned a vault for himself and his wife, Queen Elisabeth, in the Friedenskirche (Peace Church), which had been built on his instructions in the grounds of Sanssouci. This was to be the royal couple's final resting-place. However, in his will of 1854, the king had specified – this was entirely in keeping with the traditions of the Catholic princes – that his heart should be interred at the foot of his parents' tomb, in a heart-shaped container of Brandenburg granite.

In 1890, at the time of Kaiser Wilhelm II, the last extension of the Mausoleum was carried out – under the supervision of the royal surveyor-general Albert

Geyer – in order to accommodate the sarcophagi of Kaiser Wilhelm I (1797–1888) and his consort, Augusta (1811–1890). The north wall facing the entrance was shifted back by a distance equivalent to the depth of the building, and the total space was thus doubled. The monuments to the imperial couple were executed by Erdmann Encke between 1890 and 1894.

Also interred here, in the vault on the lower level of the burial chamber, are Prince Albrecht of Prussia (1809–1872), the younger brother of Friedrich Wilhelm IV, and Duchesse Auguste of Liegnitz (1800–1873), the second, morganatic consort of Friedrich Wilhelm III.

The Grounds

The few isolated changes made by Friedrich Wilhelm IV to the grounds at Charlottenburg were tentative ones. The king avoided any radical innovations and was concerned to preserve the gardens as they were, or, where he deemed it necessary, to improve them in line with the historicist taste of the times. The only salient change he made – and it was fully in accord with the original baroque character of the garden – was to restore the main avenue that cut through the beech-grove and drew the eye to the centre of the Great Orangery. This had been removed by Lenné. In the circular flower-bed to the west of the palace, Bartholomäus Eggers's 1692 statue of Minerva, which had been found armless and headless in the palace grounds, was now erected. On the orders of the king, it was restored by the sculptor August Willich, under the supervision of Rauch, and, at the king's request, it was given the features of Queen Sophie Charlotte, the founder of the palace.

It was also Friedrich Wilhelm IV who had the baroque sculptures and statues which had been removed by his father, Friedrich Wilhelm III, and Lenné, replaced in the grounds of Charlottenburg and Sanssouci. Commenting on the changes to his garden design, Lenné remarked laconically: 'Who can swim against the tide!'

The construction of the embankment for the Berlin–Hamburg railway line along the northern edge of the palace grounds, together with the increasing industrialization of the Berlin and Charlottenburg area in the middle of the nineteenth century, put an abrupt end to any notion of a landscape garden. The impression of a fluid transition from designed grounds to untamed nature was severely disrupted by increasing urbanization. The growth of the town of Charlottenburg around the palace site, with the addition of tall houses and factories, further contributed to the park's being blocked off from the surrounding area.

Lawn was added to the palace's main courtyard; and orange-trees were installed there. The only trace of the green areas that has survived is the brick edging of the central plot, on top of which Andreas Schlüter's equestrian statue of the Great Elector was placed after the Second World War.

The two Borghese Wrestlers on top of the guard-houses are cast in lead. They already formed part of the baroque garden's collection of sculpture in about 1740 and were placed here in 1802.

The Area around the Palace: Luisenplatz and Schloßallee

From early on in his reign, Friedrich Wilhelm IV was keen to alter the side of the palace facing the main courtyard. This was the location of the buildings that housed the royal stables and the stables of the Garde du Corps. Friedrich Wilhelm's plan was to add two imposing buildings that would mark out the square and the beginning of the approach to the palace. A pupil of Schinkel, Friedrich August Stüler, was commissioned to design and execute the two buildings. However, the plans could not be put in motion until autumn 1855, when the necessary land had been acquired.

The two three-storey, square buildings lie in a straight line from the palace. On all four sides they have a central projection topped with a triangular gable. The façades are sectioned by prominent Corinthian pilasters. Both buildings have a circular top structure on which stands an open round temple with cupola (monopteral). The two temple structures echo the design of the cupola on the old palace building and form the architectural link with the palace. Both buildings are currently used as museums by the Berlin Museums Authority (Staatliche Museen zu Berlin – Preußischer Kulturbesitz).

Charlottenburg Palace after 1918

When the monarchy disappeared in 1918, the fate of the eighty or so palaces, castles, and mansions which the erstwhile Prussian royal house had owned all over Germany was, to begin with, uncertain, to say the least. Many palaces were temporarily assigned to other functions; even Charlottenburg served as a military hospital at that time. As early as 1919, efforts were put in train by various well-known figures to ensure that outstanding palaces belonging to the monarchy were permanently preserved as 'important and irreplaceable tokens of German history and German artistic and cultural development' (Hans von Makowsky). In about 1926, after a lengthy period of expert discussion, there emerged the concept of the 'museum palace'; and in 1927 the Administration of State Palaces and Gardens was founded to oversee the former Prussian royal palaces. The Administration's task was to preserve and maintain the 'organic unit' into which the fifty and more palaces and castles under its jurisdiction had now grown. (Some of these also had large grounds attached to them.) The palaces concerned contained particularly valuable stocks of artistic and cultural-historical items. One of them was the palace of Charlottenburg, together with its grounds and the buildings in them.

In 1943, large parts of the palace, the Great Orangery, the Belvedere, and the New (Schinkel) Pavilion were burnt down during the second large-scale bombing-raid by the Royal Air Force. Damage continued until the end of the war.

After the war, the fate of the palace, lying in ruins amongst the rubble of the city, was at first uncertain. But as early as 1946, work began to make some of the palace rooms safe against the rigours of winter. The real reconstruction work – due in the main to the tenacity and great drive of the then director, Dr Margarete Kühn – began in 1950. A first, external phase was completed on 30 April 1956, with the positioning of Richard Scheibe's figure of Fortuna atop the restored cupola. The interior restoration took much longer, and is still not complete today (1995).

Golden Gallery from the south-west
Photographed soon after the Second World War

As early as 1952, Andreas Schlüter's sculptural masterpiece – the equestrian statue of the Great Elector, commissioned by Friedrich I – was installed in the middle of the main courtyard of Charlottenburg Palace. Its original location, from 1703, was the Lange Brücke close by the Royal Palace. The bronze statue, which had been removed during the war, had been submerged in the Tegeler See and was not salvaged until 1949.

As far as Charlottenburg's post-war history is concerned, one has to remember that because of the division of Germany, and because of the redistribution of the former Prussian territories, the great Prussian institution of the Administration of State Palaces and Gardens lost all its palaces except for Potsdam-Sanssouci, Charlottenburg with the Pfaueninsel Castle, and Grunewald, which were located on West German territory. As a result of the Iron Curtain, however, two distinct palace-administrations grew up.

One big problem was the question of the furniture and fittings. The art objects from the various palaces had for the most part been evacuated to other places during the war, and after the end of hostilities Charlottenburg was only able to recover items located on the territory of the Western Allies. The art objects that had been transferred to the eastern part of Germany, or to the Soviet zone, were no longer accessible to the palaces in West Berlin. In addition, at many of the

108

storage-places, items were destroyed or carried off. Since German reunification –
and particularly since the former Prussian palaces in Berlin and Potsdam were
brought together, in 1995, to form the Foundation of Prussian Palaces and Garden
in Berlin-Brandenburg (Stiftung Preußische Schlösser und Gärten Berlin-
Brandenburg) – a brisk exchange of furnishings and fittings has been possible,
and Charlottenburg Palace has in its turn been recovering valuable items of its
original furniture and fittings. TK

Lower Oval Hall and Upper Oval Hall viewed to the
south, April 1949

Palace chapel, looking south, April 1949

The Crown Treasure

The most recent innovation in Charlottenburg Palace has been the setting-up, in 1995, of a Crown Treasure Room, in which the remains of the Hohenzollern crown treasure are exhibited. This adjoins the Silver Treasury. The first Crown Treasure Room had been set up by Friedrich I after 1701 in his apartments in the Royal Palace. The royal architect Eosander had designed four corner display-cupboards of carved walnut in which the objects were stored. When the Hohenzollern Museum was installed in Monbijou after 1877, this small square Treasure Room was reconstructed and the original ceiling restored. The third Treasure Room that has now been opened in Charlottenburg is designed as a museum area. In it are preserved the gold mounts of the crowns used by Friedrich I and Sophie Charlotte at the coronation of 1701, together with the late seventeenth-century gold sceptre adapted for the same coronation. The room also contains the 1701 orb and Friedrich I's imperial seal. Also on display are the Prussian electoral sword, originally a consecrated sword which Pope Pius II gave to Margrave Albrecht Achilles of Brandenburg on 6 January 1460 in Mantua, and the original Prussian ducal sword, drawn by Jobst Freudener for the first secular duke of Prussia, Albrecht, in Königsberg in 1540–1. From 1701 the ducal sword had served as the imperial sword of the kings of Prussia. Also included in the crown treasure are the funerary helmet of the Great Elector, created for his funeral in 1688, and an iron chest with lock, dating from the time of Friedrich I and in which the crown treasure was at one time stored.

A collar of the Order of the Black Eagle recalls the foundation of this prestigious Prussian order on the eve of the coronation of 1701 in Königsberg. As a complement to this the display includes the silver-gilt coats of arms of the first three bearers of the Prussian ducal sword, together with a silver-gilt medallion bearing a portrait of Duke Albrecht and his consort, Dorothea. A very welcome addition to the collection is the gold key given by the Great Elector to the chamberlain of the dukedom of Stettin-Hinterpommern in 1655 (on loan from a private collection).   WB

Funerary helmet
Copper, beaten, fire-gilt
Berlin, 1688
Originally made for the funeral of the Great Elector in 1688 and subsequently carried, together with the imperial insignia, at the funeral processions of all male members of the royal house.

Imperial seal
Iron, engraved
Medallist: Samuel Stall
Berlin, 1700
The imperial seal, closely associated with the royal insignia, bears the stamp of Friedrich I.
Silver-gilt container by the Berlin goldsmith Humbert & Son, mid-19th century

Mounts of crowns of Friedrich I and Sophie Charlotte
Gold, enamel
Berlin, 1700
These solid gold mounts were made for the coronation
of Friedrich I as 'King in Prussia' in Königsberg in
1701. The 1713 inventory drawn up as part of
Friedrich I's will lists 153 'facet stones' (diamonds) and
brilliants and 8 drop-pearls for the king's crown, and
147 'facet stones', 25 brilliants, 8 drop-pearls and
48 round pearls for the queen's. The jewels were not
permanently fixed; they were removed and used
'elsewhere' by the queens.

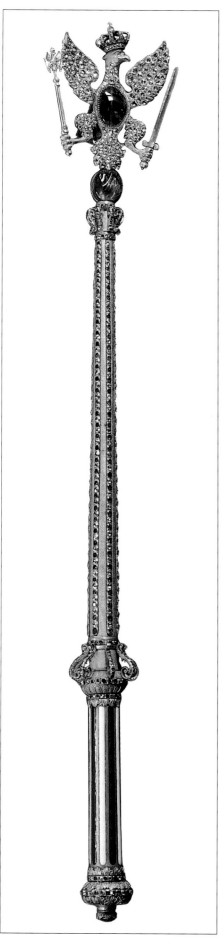

Sceptre belonging to Friedrich I
Unknown goldsmith, Berlin (?), *c.* 1700
The eagle's body is formed of a magnificent ruby
which Tsar Peter the Great is reputed to have given to
the Elector, later King Friedrich I, on the occasion of a
visit to Königsberg in 1697

Ducal sword of Albrecht of Prussia, later imperial
sword of Prussia
Hilt and blade: silver, gilded
Goldsmith: Jobst Freudener (Ulm)
Königsberg, 1540–1
Lent by the House of Hohenzollern

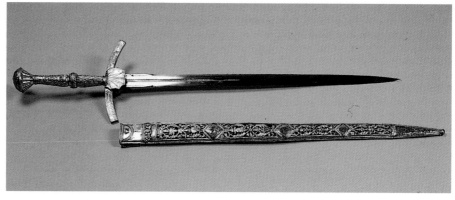

Consecrated sword of Margrave, later Elector Albrecht
Achilles, used since the 16th century as the electoral
sword of Brandenburg
Hilt and blade: silver, gilded
Goldsmith: Simone de Martino
Florence, before 1460
Lent by the House of Hohenzollern

The Silver Treasury

The importance of the culinary regime in the history of a royal household – a subject that has attracted much attention in recent research – cannot be overestimated. The royal table played an important part, within court ceremonial, in demonstrating a ruler's magnificence. For the king, the giving of the coronation feast signified his taking possession of his kingdom; and for those who participated, it signified their express acknowledgement of him.

The development of the silver treasury – or, as it is more appropriately called in the Vienna Hofburg, the 'Hofsilber- und Tafelkammer' (tableware and silver treasury) – was the fruit of a long tradition linked to the increased expenditure on tableware which occurred as a result of the growing importance of court and culinary ceremonial from the sixteenth century. The major palaces of the Hohenzollerns also had their silver cabinets. For practical reasons, these were generally located near the royal kitchens, and this is true of Charlottenburg at the time of the monarchy. Silver treasuries were, in the most precise sense, depositories for precious tableware; they accommodated silver buffets, and were used to store the many *Huldigungsgeschenke* or 'gifts of allegiance' that were generally presented on the occasion of accessions or, in particular, at weddings. Older tableware was decommissioned – generally after long years of use – and the material was used to produce new ware. The golden age of the Brandenburg-Prussian silver treasuries is considered to be the time of Friedrich III, who acceded to the throne as Friedrich I in 1701. The silverware inventory of this first Prussian king alone lists eleven silver services, including a silver-gilt one; in addition there were three sets of silver kitchenware. In addition to the usual melting-down to create new services, most of the Hohenzollern silver disappeared in the meltings that took place during Frederick the Great's Silesian Wars, and in the patriotic 'gold for iron' campaign conducted during the Napoleonic occupation of Prussia in 1809.

At the close of the imperial age, only a small part of the seventeenth- and eighteenth-century collections from the Silver Treasury survived. One exception was the famous Augsburg buffet in the Rittersaal at the Royal Palace. The only eighteenth-century silver service to have survived the meltings was that belonging to Frederick the Great, created by Johann Christian Lieberkühn the Younger. After 1918, only the silver buffet remained in the Royal Palace; the remainder of the silver collection from that palace accompanied Kaiser Wilhelm II into exile to Huis Doorn (near Utrecht) in Holland.

After 1945 the remaining Hohenzollern palaces in the care of the Administration of State Palaces and Gardens in Potsdam and West Berlin no longer contained any royal silver. The creation of a modest Silver Treasury in Charlottenburg Palace

The Crown Prince's Silver
Berlin, 1904–14
The Crown Prince's Silver, comprising 2,694 pieces for 50 place-settings, was a gift presented by 414 Prussian cities to the last Prussian crown prince, Wilhelm (1882–1951) and his consort, Cecilie Duchess of Mecklenburg-Schwerin (1886–1954), on the occasion of their marriage. Most of the figural *surtouts* are by Ignatius Taschner (1871–1913), and the utensils are by Emil Lettré (1876–1954).

Willkomm cup in the shape of a boy Bacchant
Silver, parcel gilt
Goldsmith: Hans Lambrecht
Hamburg, *c.* 1660
This boy Bacchant, formerly part of the table silver
belonging to the Great Elector, is a particularly
magnificent example of the Hamburg goldsmith's art,
which attained its heyday in the second half of the
17th century. A *Willkomm* cup is a drinking-vessel
designed to be passed round large companies of
guests.

in 1993 was made possible by the kind co-operation of the Stichting Huis Doorn in Holland – which loaned Charlottenburg various items from the former royal collections – and by a number of spectacular purchases of historical silver items from Hohenzollern collections, made possible by help from a variety of sponsors: the Deutsche Bank Berlin, the Ernst von Siemens-Kunstfonds Munich, the Deutsche Klassenlotterie Berlin, Esso Hamburg, and the Klingbeil-Gruppe Berlin.

As a result, silver objects from the time of the Great Elector (1640–88), of Friedrich III/I (ruled 1688–1713), and of the Soldier King, Friedrich Wilhelm I, are once again on display in Charlottenburg. The Silver Treasury also includes pieces from Frederick the Great's Lieberkühn table-silver, items belonging to Friedrich Wilhelm II (ruled 1786–97) and Friedrich Wilhelm III (1797–1840), and parts of a set of table decoration created for the Prince of Prussia, Prince William, later King and Kaiser Wilhelm I (ruled 1861–88).

Terrine from Friedrich II's table service
Silver
Marked: LIEBERKÜHN
Berlin, 1746–7
The terrine betrays Parisian influence. The exuberantly executed vine-shoots perhaps indicate that the service was used in the 'Weinbergschloß' (Vigne) Sanssouci.

Since 1995 one room has been devoted to the last example of Hohenzollern table-silver, presented by 414 Prussian towns to the royal couple Wilhelm and Cecilie in 1905 on the occasion of their marriage. This extensive table-service, which originally comprised 2,694 pieces and was not completed until 1914, is the last example of great royal silverware in the twentieth century (on loan from the regional authorities of Berlin).

When, in the eighteenth century, the triumphant rise of porcelain challenged the supremacy of silver on royal tables, the great porcelain tableware also made its way into the silver treasuries. Then, in about 1800, the great French fire-gilt bronze *surtout-de-tables* in vogue at that time began to appear, inspiring German workshops to produce their own designs.

One area in the Silver Treasury is devoted to the porcelain tableware made for Frederick the Great in the Meissen manufactory and the Berlin KPM. Between 1765 and 1786 Friedrich commissioned twenty-one services for the royal palaces from the KPM alone; some of these were executed to his own, very precise designs. Also on show in this area is a service commissioned for Frederick the Great by the Preußisch-Asiatische Compagnie. Another Huis Doorn exhibit is the highly architectural bronze fire-gilt Berlin table-decoration made by Karl Friedrich Schinkel for Friedrich Wilhelm III. WB

Münzhumpen (tankard inset with coins)
Silver, gilded inside
Goldsmith: Daniel Männlich the Elder (1625–1701)
Berlin, shortly after 1692
This magnificent exemplar of the Berlin *Münzhumpen*,
topped with the Brandenburg electoral cap, is for the
most part uniformly decorated with thaler coins issued
to commemorate the swearing of the oath of alle-
giance by the city of Magdeburg (17 October 1692).
Lent by the Huis Doorn Foundation (Netherlands)

Round dish and dessert plate from Frederick the
Great's 'Japanese Service'
Meissen, c. 1763
Designed to the detailed specifications of the king,
who supplied a French silver plate as a model.
The name of the service was prompted by the exotic
animal design.
Lent by the Freunde der Preußischen Schlösser und
Gärten

Items from the table service with 'Prussian musical
design'
Meissen, c. 1761
This extensive service, made to specifications drawn up
by Friedrich II and intended for his own personal use,
came into the possession of General von Möllendorf
(1724–1816) as a gift in 1783.
Purchased with assistance from the Ernst von Siemens-
Kunstfonds (Munich)

Museum of the History
of Berlin Porcelain
(in the Belvedere)

any of the European porcelain manufactories of the eighteenth century have, in the course of time, had an opportunity of illustrating the history of their output in a museum which they themselves have set up. For the Königliche Porzellan-Manufaktur (KPM – Royal Porcelain Manufactory), that moment did not arrive until 1971, when the Berlin Senate, aided by the Deutsche Klassenlotterie Berlin, acquired the private collection of Karl-Heinz Bröhan. The reconstructed Belvedere, the interior decoration of which had not been restored, offered the ideal setting for a display of this kind. Responsibility for maintaining and extending the collection was entrusted to the Administration of State Palaces and Gardens.

Given that this was to be a museum relating to a porcelain manufactory that was still in existence, the regional authorities of Berlin had a considerable interest in using it to help secure the future of the KPM. From the outset, the Berlin porcelain collection in the Belvedere had two basic purposes. The first was to provide the public with an *aperçu* of the output of this, the only eighteenth-century Berlin workshop to have operated without a break up to the present time, and, as a concomitant to this, to bring the name of the KPM, rich in tradition, into greater public focus. In addition, the collection was to serve as a source of inspiration for KPM craftsmen.

The systematic extension of the collection since 1971 – attributable in large measure to the generous support of the Stiftung Deutsche Klassenlotterie Berlin – has meant that what was initially a small collection has now grown into a respectably sized museum, and one that has managed to satisfy expectations in regard to this recently established institution. The collection currently includes one of the largest stocks of porcelain from the first Prussian porcelain manufactory in Berlin, a private company founded by Wilhelm Caspar Wegely which operated from 1751 to 1757. The second private company – that of Johann Ernst Gotzkowsky – which operated between 1761 and 1763 and, within this short period, managed to produce some outstanding items, is also excellently illustrated in the Belvedere collection. Gotzkowsky's company formed the basis for the later KPM.

The focal point of the collection, however, is the porcelain produced by the KPM from 1763. Because of the shortage of space, the display confines itself to giving a historical overview, essentially up to the Biedermeier period. No such limits apply to acquisitions, which extend to the present day.

In 1981, when the city was still divided, the historical archives relating to the Porcelain Manufactory were handed over by East Berlin (GDR) to West Berlin. At that point it was decided that these archives should be housed in Charlotten-

Boy with Birds
Wegely Manufactory, c. 1755
The figure is inspired by the character of 'Corydon' in the ballet-pantomime *La Vallée de Montmorency ou Les Amours villageoises* by the French librettist Favart (1710–92). The immediate model for it is a porcelain figure from Vincennes based on a design by François Boucher (1703–70).

burg Palace. Using these as a basis, it has been possible to organize a whole series of special exhibitions on the history of the Manufactory – a fitting adjunct to this particular museographical mission.

The KPM's history not only provides ample justification of its right to bear a royal title; it also documents the role of individual monarchs as major clients and awarders of commissions. Thanks to these many, and often expensive, special commissions, the Manufactory's output regularly approached the highest standards of the great European porcelain manufactories. The Prussian monarchs had a decisive influence on the artistic quality and style of the output of their Manufactory. Without this commitment on the part of the royal house, the fate of the Manufactory, like that of many other European porcelain-workshops, would have been sealed long ago. The special historical role thus played by the Prussian

Cup and saucer with Chinese-style decoration
after Watteau
KPM, c. 1768

monarchs in encouraging enterprise and setting standards of quality makes the accommodation of this Museum of the History of Berlin Porcelain on the site of a former royal palace particularly fitting. And since the Royal Porcelain Manufactory still has its workshops in the Charlottenburg district, the choice of the palace grounds as a location for the Museum was an obvious one. WB

Pieces from a coffee-service with painted flower-design
en terrasse
KPM, *c.* 1790

Pieces from a tea-service with design of imitation of
mosaic and precious stones
KPM, *c.* 1810

Page 124:
Large *potpourri* vase with sculpted reed-leaves and
roses painted with 'flying children *en grisaille*',
after Boucher
KPM, *c.* 1768–70

Krater-vase with eagle-shaped handles and *bisquit*
portrait of Friedrich Wilhelm III by Leonhard Posch
(1750–1831)
KPM, 1817

Vase sculpture
Model by Gottlieb Elster (1867–1917)
KPM, 1899

Vase with staggered coloured ovals
Decoration by Ernst Böhm (1890–1963)

Genealogy of the Prussian Royal House

Friedrich Wilhelm of Brandenburg
the Great Elector *1620 †1688 El. 1640
1. ⚭ Louisa Henrietta of Orange *1627 †1667
2. ⚭ Dorothea of Holstein-Glücksburg *1636 †1689

Friedrich III *1657 †1713 El. 1688
Friedrich I, 'King in Prussia', 1701
1. ⚭ Elisabeth Henriette of Hessen-Kassel *1661 †1685
2. ⚭ Sophie Charlotte of Hanover *1668 †1705
3. ⚭ Sofie Luise of Mecklenburg-Schwerin *1685 †1735

Friedrich Wilhelm I
*1688 †1740 Kg. 1713
'Soldier King'
⚭ Sophie Dorothea of Hanover
*1687 †1757

Friedrich
*1707 †1708

Wilhelmine Friederike
Sophie
*1709 †1758
⚭ Friedrich Mg. of
Brandenburg-Bayreuth
*1711 †1763

Elisabeth Friederike of
Brandenburg-Bayreuth
*1732 †1780
⚭ Karl II of Württemberg
*1728 †1793

Friedrich II
the Great
*1712 †1786
Kg. 1740
⚭ Elisabeth
Christine of
Braunschweig-
Bevern
*1715 †1797

Friederike Luise
*1714 †1784
⚭ Karl Mg. of
Brandenburg-
Ansbach
*1712 †1757

Philippine Charlotte
*1716 †1801
⚭ Karl I Duke of
Braunschweig-
Wolfenbüttel
*1713 †1780

Karl II Wilhelm
Ferdinand
*1735 †1806
⚭ Augusta 'von
Großbritannien'
*1737 †1813

Sophie
*1719 †1765
⚭ Friedrich Wilhelm
Mg. of Brandenburg-
Schwedt
*1700 †1771

Luise Ulrike
*1720 †1782
⚭ Adolf Friedrich
Kg. of Sweden
*1710 †1771

Gustav III
*1746 †1792
⚭ Sophie Magdalene
of Denmark
*1746 †1813

August Wilhelm
*1722 †1758
⚭ Luise Amalie
of Braunschweig-
Wolfenbüttel
*1722 †1780

Friedrich Wilhelm II
*1744 †1797
Kg. 1786
1. ⚭ Friederike Luise of
Braunschweig-Wolfenbüttel
*1746 †1840
2. ⚭ Friederike Luise
of Hessen-Darmstadt
*1751 †1805

Amalie
*1723 †1787
Abbess in Quedlinburg
1755

Heinrich
*1726 †1802
⚭ Wilhelmine
of Hessen-Kassel
*1726 †1808

Ferdinand
*1730 †1813
⚭ Luise of Brandenburg-
Schwedt
*1738 †1820

Friedrich Wilhelm III
*1770 †1840 Kg. 1797
1. ⚭ Luise of Mecklenburg-Strelitz
*1776 †1810
2. ⚭ Auguste of Harrach
*1800 †1873

Friedrich Wilhelm IV
*1795 †1861 Kg. 1840
⚭ Elisabeth of Bavaria
*1801 †1873

Wilhelm I
*1797 †1888
Kg. 1861
(regent 1858)
1871 emperor of Germany
⚭ Augusta of Saxony-
Weimar
*1811 †1890

Wilhelm
*1785 †1851
⚭ Marie Anna of Hessen-Homburg
*1785 †1846

Marie
*1825 †1889
⚭ Maximilian II
Kg. of Bavaria
*1811 †1864

Friedrich III
*1831 †1888 emperor 1888
(Crown Prince Friedrich Wilhelm)
⚭ Victoria, P.R. of Great Britain
*1840 †1901

Ludwig II
*1845 †1886
Kg. of Bavaria 1864

Otto I
*1848 †1916
Kg. 1886

Wilhelm II
*1859 †1941 emperor 1888–1918
1. ⚭ Auguste Viktoria
of Holstein-Augustenburg
*1858 †1921
2. ⚭ Hermine Reuß
*1887 †1947

Wilhelm
*1882 †1951
⚭ Cecilie of Mecklenburg-Schwerin
*1886 †1954

KEY
El. *Elector*
Kg. *King*
Mg. *Margrave*
P.R. *Princess Royal*

125

Bibliography

Die Architektur der deutschen Schlösser. II. Das Königliche Schloß zu Charlottenburg, Hermann Rückwardt (ed.), Berlin 1894

Backschat, Friedrich, 'Neues zur Geschichte der Schloßbesitzung Charlottenburg', in: *Mitteilungen des Vereins für die Geschichte Berlins* 50, 1933, pp. 46–48

Baer, Winfried, *Berliner Porzellan vom Rokoko bis Biedermeier*, Berlin [1970]

Baer, Winfried, *Berliner Porzellan aus dem Belvedere / Schloß Charlottenburg*, Berlin 1989

Baer, Winfried, *Prunktabatièren Friedrichs des Großen*, exh. cat., Potsdam–Sanssouci 1993

Baer, Winfried and Ilse Baer, *... auf Allerhöchsten Befehl ... Königsgeschenke aus der Königlichen Porzellan-Manufaktur Berlin – KPM*, Berlin 1984

Baer, Winfried and Ilse Baer, *Blumen für den König. 225 Jahre Breslauer Stadtschloß-Service*, exh. cat., Berlin 1992

Baer, Winfried, Ilse Baer and Suzanne Grosskopf-Knaack, *Von Gotzkowsky zur KPM. Aus der Frühzeit friderizianischen Porzellans*, exh. cat., Berlin 1986

Beger, Lorenz, *Thesaurus Brandenburgicus ...*, Berlin 1696

Biederstedt, Rudolf, *Johann Friedrich Eosander, Grundzüge einer Biographie*, (Kungl. Vitterhets Historie och Antikvitetsakademien. Antikvariskt Arkiv 17) Stockholm 1961

Börsch-Supan, Helmut, *Marmorsaal und Blaues Zimmer. So wohnen Fürsten*, Berlin 1976

Börsch-Supan, Helmut, *Die Werke Christian Daniel Rauchs im Schloßbezirk von Charlottenburg*, Berlin 1977

Börsch-Supan, Helmut, *Die Werke Carl Blechens im Schinkel-Pavillon*, Berlin 1978

Börsch-Supan, Helmut, *Die Kunst in Brandenburg-Preußen. Ihre Geschichte von der Renaissance bis zum Biedermeier dargestellt am Kunstbesitz der Berliner Schlösser*, Berlin 1980

Börsch-Supan, Helmut, *Das Mausoleum im Charlottenburger Schloßgarten*, Berlin ²1981

Börsch-Supan, Helmut, *Der Schinkel-Pavillon im Schloßpark zu Charlottenburg*, Berlin ⁵1990

Börsch-Supan, Helmut, Tilo Eggeling and Martin Sperlich, *Der Weiße Saal und die Goldene Galerie im Schloß Charlottenburg*, Berlin 1973

Broebes, Jean-Baptiste, *Vues des Palais et Maisons de Plaisance de Sa Majesté le Roy de Prusse*, Augsburg 1733

Eckhardt, Götz, 'Zweites Rokoko um 1840 in den königlichen Schlössern von Berlin und Potsdam', in: *Historismus – Aspekte zur Kunst im 19. Jahrhundert*, hg. Karl-Heinz Klingenburg, Leipzig 1985, pp. 141–156

Eggeling, Tilo, *Die Wohnungen Friedrichs des Großen im Schloß Charlottenburg*, Berlin 1978

Eggeling, Tilo, *Studien zum friderizianischen Rokoko. Georg Wenceslaus von Knobelsdorff als Entwerfer von Innendekorationen*, Berlin 1980

Eggeling, Tilo, Regina Hanemann and Jürgen Julier, *Ein Schloß in Trümmern. Charlottenburg im November 1943*, Berlin 1993

Gundlach, Wilhelm, *Geschichte der Stadt Charlottenburg*, 2 vol., Berlin 1905

Julier, Jürgen, 'Die Große Orangerie des Charlottenburger Schlosses', in: *Der Bär von Berlin*, 1991

Königliche Schlösser in Berlin-Brandenburg, Hans-Joachim Giersberg and Jürgen Julier (ed.), Berlin–Potsdam 1993

Kühn, Margarete, *Schloß Charlottenburg*, Berlin 1955

Kühn, Margarete, *Schloß Charlottenburg. Die Bauwerke und Kunstdenkmäler von Berlin*, 2 vol., Berlin 1970

Nicolai, Friedrich, *Beschreibung der Königlichen Residenzstädte Berlin und Potsdam und aller daselbst befindlichen Merkwürdigkeiten*, Berlin, 1769, 1779, 1786

Österreich, Matthias, *Description de tout l'Intérieur des Deux Palais de Sanssouci, de ceux de Potsdam et de Charlottenbourg*, Berlin 1773

Österreich, Matthias, *Beschreibung aller Seltenheiten der Kunst und übrigen Alterthümer; besonders an Statuen in dem Königl. Lustschlosse Charlottenburg bey der Residenz-Stadt Berlin*, Berlin 1768

Oettingen, Wolfgang von, 'Die bildenden Künste unter König Friedrich I. 1. Die königliche Akademie der Künste', in: *Hohenzollern-Jahrbuch* 4, 1900, pp. 231–246

Peschken, Goerd, 'Andreas Schlüter und das Schloß Charlottenburg', in: *Schloß Charlottenburg. Berlin. Preußen, Festschrift für Margarete Kühn*, Martin Sperlich and Helmut Börsch-Supan (ed.), Munich–Berlin 1975

Preußische Königsschlösser in Berlin und Potsdam, Hans-Joachim Giersberg and Jürgen Julier (ed.), Leipzig 1992

Reidemeister, Leopold, 'Die Porzellankabinette der brandenburgisch-preußischen Schlösser', in: *Jahrbuch der Preußischen Kunstsammlungen* 54, 1933, pp. 262–272; 55, 1934, pp. 42–56

Rumpf, Johann Daniel Friedrich, *Beschreibung der äußern und innern Merkwürdigkeiten der Königlichen Schlösser in Berlin, Charlottenburg, Schönhausen, in den bei Potsdam*, 1794

Sachs, Curt, *Musik und Oper am Kurbrandenburgischen Hof*, Hildesheim–New York 1977

Karl Friedrich Schinkel. Architektur – Malerei – Kunstgewerbe, exh. cat., Berlin 1981

Seidel, Paul, 'Der Neue Flügel Friedrichs des Großen am Charlottenburger Schloß', in: *Hohenzollern-Jahrbuch* 16, 1912, pp. 86–94

Seidel, Paul, 'Die bildenden Künste unter Friedrich I. Teil 2: Kunst und Künstler am Hofe', in: *Hohenzollern-Jahrbuch* 4, 1900, pp. 247–268

Sophie Charlotte und die Musik in Lietzenburg, ed. by the Staatliches Institut für Musikforschung Preußischer Kulturbesitz, Berlin 1987

Sperlich, Martin, *Schloß Charlottenburg*, Berlin 1974

Theatrum Europaeum, XVI, 1703, [Frankfurt/Main] 1717

Voss, Georg, 'Das Königliche Schloß zu Charlottenburg', in: *Mitteilungen des Vereins für die Geschichte Berlins* 15, pp. 120–124

Wimmer, Clemens Alexander, *Die Gärten des Charlottenburger Schlosses*, Berlin 1985

Detail of the railings of the main courtyard with the star of the Order of the Black Eagle

The objective of the series *Museen, Schlösser und Denkmäler in Deutschland* is the promotion of the arts.
BANQUE PARIBAS has a long-standing commitment to art sponsorship.
Its aim is to enhance understanding and appreciation of the arts, including the treasures of Germany's museums and castles.
The series covering the Federal Republic is supported by
BANQUE PARIBAS (DEUTSCHLAND) OHG.

Books in print:

Leipzig, Museum of Fine Arts
Schwerin, Staatliches Museum – Collections, Castles and Gardens

The series *Museen, Schlösser und Denkmäler in Deutschland* is published by Fonds Mercator Paribas on behalf of Musées et Monuments de France.

© Musées et Monuments de France 1995
ISBN (paperback) 2-907333-92-5
ISBN (hardback) 2-907333-93-3

Photography by
   Jörg Anders, Berlin
   Fotostudio Bartsch, Berlin
   Bart Cloet, Ghent
   Hirmer, Munich
   Mauritius, Berlin
   Ullstein, Berlin
Translated by Margaret Clarke, Oxford
Editing: Barbara Gaehtgens, Berlin
Design: Antoon De Vijlder, Zandhoven

Printed in Belgium